For Still We Hear Them Singing

By Robert E Pike

Photographs
by
Carrie Pike

Grosvenor House
Publishing Limited

This book is published by
Grosvenor House Publishing Ltd
28-30 High Street, Guildford, Surrey, GU1 3EL.
www.grosvenorhousepublishing.co.uk

A CIP record for this book
is available from the British Library

ISBN 978-1-78148-911-6

These poems are dedicated to the memory of my mother and father; to the pretty French war-widow in silk stockings who was caught on camera and inspired my first poem, and to my special family, Carrie, Ben, Sam, Kate and two wonderful additions, my daughter-in-law, Kate and my grandson Jacob, in the profound hope that he will never have to 'march away.'

Introduction

As a child I lived in the same house as my maternal grandfather, on the mantelpiece were the cases of two brass shells, and a small 'goblet' made of different-sized bullets; they fascinated me, but I never asked where they came from. After he died two medals came my way and for years sat in my drawer, unnoticed.

At school I loved English and inevitably Owen & Sassoon came into my cosmos, then the epiphany occurred. My parents on holiday bought me the diary of an officer in the Somerset Light Infantry, Geoffrey Prideaux, which I devoured. Next year meandering in France we decided to find where he was buried and after much difficulty found Hem Farm with the added interest of two VCs, and the obsession stretched and stirred. If Prideaux, why not Owen and next summer we went to Ors; no reassuring CWGC signs showed us to the Communal Cemetery, so we went to the Mairie to ask where the famous 'poète anglais' was buried. 'Qui?' was the response; they were unaware of who they had, not so today!

Then fate took control I had to give up the job; became an apron-decked house-husband, but found when the children were at school, what to do? I looked at the town war memorial and its 159 names, a research project, easy, I thought. Ten years later I found the 159th, Walter Hill, lying unmarked, forgotten in the town cemetery and the task, except for the small matter of a book, was complete.

* * *

Meanwhile Grandad's medals were framed, a Dead Man's Penny discovered, a Military Cross like Owen's was bought and the never-ending pilgrimage began. I was intrigued by who had died in the Great War; the effect on individuals, relatives, society, suddenly the men who had lived in my town were comrades in sacrifice with Test cricketers, sons of lords and politicians, actors, poets, scions of industry, society and simply the brave.

Once this plethora of potential research emerged the future was inevitable – the Pike caravanserai inexorably explored Flanders, Asiago, Salonika, Germany, Israel and Gallipoli – Oh Gallipoli, once seen, a part of one's soul forever, the sea, the flowers, the tragedy.

Visiting these places was enhanced by the books, particularly the poems, but throughout it all there was an underlying sense that there but for the Grace of...... I looked at my two sons and thanked God they were born when they were,

For me it will always be the Great War; a war about people, not strategy, statistics, battles. I decided once to research brothers who had died, tragic, but then realised it was commonplace, so much so that now I realise even three brothers really is!

Questions haunt me – how many parents died of grief; how do you choose an inscription for your beloved son's headstone, surely the most important phrase you ever write; what would society be like if the intellectuals, poets, politicians had not died? I inevitably return to Grandads, both of whom returned, but not unscathed, one, 'a verray gentil parfit knyght' in every way, took, for a short time, to drink, the other became a miserable b....; lives were never the same and not long after another despot needed 'sorting' and their sons obliged.

It is easy to idealise the plucky Tommy withstanding the rampaging Boche hordes, but these were ordinary men – men who lived in any road, any town; men who were far from Classical heroes; far from supermen; not perfect or idealised, just caught in a moment of time where they felt they had to do their duty out of patriotism, or fear, love, necessity, under duress – who knows?

To write about the Great War is a voyage into the human suffering it embedded in the fabric of every participant country. For those who lost a loved one a light had been extinguished, never to be rekindled. For those who did return, many had physical and psychological scars. These could not fade away – they were the legacy of a war that ended only with their deaths or the deaths of those who loved them. *"What can the world hold afterwards worthy of laughter or tears?"*

For me the catalysts for the need to write poetry were three-fold -the purchase of a home in Authuille, at the heart of the Somme battlefield, beneath the looming presence of the Thiepval Memorial to the Missing and on the banks of the river Ancre beloved by Blunden, a rural paradise yet redolent with pain and sacrifice. Here on a summer's morning every July at 7 a.m. one can hear the whistles blow across the fields from Lochnagar and the ghosts of thousands of men rise out of the trenches and steadily walk, unwavering to their death. My first visit to Gallipoli, set between the blue of the Aegean and the Dardanelles, a stone's throw from Troy, peopled by the phantoms left behind amidst the wild flowers and fragrant herbs and the small matter of a photograph of a pretty French girl in silk stockings standing on the remains of a destroyed bunker on a pilgrimage to Fort Vaux, Verdun in 1925.

There are many dear friends who have encouraged and inspired, sometimes unknowingly, my writing whom I cannot thank enough, Pete Hobson and Rose, John and Carol King, the irrepressible Jason Diggons and Sarah, Keeley and Keegan, Karen and Sohrab, Jon and Ann Legg, George and Sarah Huxford, David and May, Brian and Janice, Matt and Johanna, Jennie Stringer, Eric and Ozlem in Gallipoli and our neighbours here and in France, Tanya and Mick.

The suffering of that noble generation has also introduced me to many new, dear comrades, notably through the campsite at Authuille, France and Essex WFA, the late beloved Jim Fallon and his wife, Clarice, the incomparable, ageless Barry and Sylvia Cuttell, Barrie and Patricia Butler, Frances and Mike Speakman, Gill and Malcolm Giles, Louise and Martin.

My thanks go also to Philippe Gorczynski, the discoverer of Deborah, the tank at Flesquieres, for allowing me to show her to you in her full glory, my brother-in-law, Ken Sinyard for his expertise and encouragement and my beloved sister, Ellen.

Finally the support of my brilliant photographer, my proof-reader, the mother of my wonderful children, Ben, Sam and Kate, my dearest friend and the love of my life, Carrie.

*La souffrance de cette noble génération m'a permis de faire la connaissance de beaucoup de nouveaux amis, principalement au camping Bellevue à Authuille.

Les amis du village d'Authuille, Jean-Claude Desailly, ses parents, M. et Mme. Desailly, Fabrice Cauchefer, Raymond et Monique, Fabrice et Nathalie et surtout, l'immense caractère d'Étienne qu'on n'oubliera jamais, nos charmants voisins Jean-Pierre et Christiane et enfin, le chef renommé en Picardie, et nos chers amis, Denis et Françoise Bourgogne.

Cet oeuvre aurait été impossible sans le support et l'aide de mon épouse qui a pris toutes les photos, fait toutes les épreuves de texte, la mère de nos enfants chéris, Ben, Sam et Kate, et l'amour de ma vie, ma chère Carrie.

I leave the last words to Sassoon, "*Have you forgotten yet?...... Look up, and swear by the green of the Spring that you'll never forget-*"

** THE VICTOR HEROES by ROBERT PIKE Published by Ancre Publishers 2000 ISBN 0-9539507-0-0.

The poems are produced in alphabetical order apart from the first and the last. Silk Stockings is where it all began and The Village Wedding was written to celebrate the marriage of my son Ben to Kate Emery. It seemed appropriate to end this anthology on a note of hope, of peace and of love.

Silk Stockings

In her haste to climb the pile of rubble
She almost tore her silk stockings,
Stopped by her clumsiness she turned to
the photographer
In hope and expectation;
Hope he had missed her inelegance,
Expectation he had caught her prettiness.
Momentarily pleased by the result
She guiltily remembered where she was
And turned shyly away.

It was here the sunlit dream faded;
Here by this crumpled pill-box
An errant 5,9 had obliterated all
his future and hers.
He had bought the silk stockings in Amiens
And they had arrived with the
briefest of love letters
The final missive of their doomed love.

1

Two days later the telegram.
In her regret at being informed she sought
comfort in his clothes,
Breathing in the slightest odour of his being
Until forgotten, dishevelled in a corner
She saw the silk stockings
The last semblance of his love.

Now a year later on the pilgrimage
The search for solace, peace, a finality
She had worn them again
Feeling a tremor of desire at their sensuality
Guiltily erotic in a place where dreams were demolished
And then she had nearly snagged them
on senile barbed wire
And all her memories would have been torn to shreds –
Silk stockings

Image for 'Silk Stockings' courtesy of
Paul Reed, Sommecourt Archives

40 Hommes Et 8 Chevaux

'Forty bloody men, not f..king likely,
Not unless they're them bleedin' bantams.'
Nobody took any notice of the gabby one,
They were too tired, it was too early, too cold –
Anyway he was the joke, never engaging
mouth and brain.
Once inside the wagon the stench of horse shit
Overwhelmed them all; soiled hay upon the floor
In the dark corners a malodorous bucket,
Another 'eau potable' completed the
first-class accommodation.'

Fresh off the heaving packet, a short march
To an anonymous siding and this
transport of delight –
One stop, the front, the terminus – Death.
Already the distant drumbeat of shell-fire
As an interminable hospital train limped by,
Drawn, pale faces etched with pain at every window.

Suddenly their ancient locomotive wheezed and creaked,
Started with an impatient jolt, throwing men off balance
Blasting smoke and cinders into faces inquisitive to leave,
Whilst most had laid down, closed heavy eyes,
'Next stop, Blackpool,' quipped the irrepressible gabby one,
No-one laughed, sleep had already gathered them in
As the train continued it slothful way to Poperinghe.

A Moment at Thiepval

Bestriding the bloody ridge
Storm clouds suddenly parted and the brick colossus
Smouldered in the dying summer sun.
Flags casually limp
Not a breath stirred to agitate their rest.
In the shadows of the passionless piers
Names slept untroubled by peering pilgrims,
Eagerly searching for a name
Do not worry, there are enough!
There is a name remembered for everyone;
Names long forgotten but for this eternal register;
Compiled on bravery, on fear, on loss.

For time immemorial a place of peace, of safety,
A home till the invader's unbridled ambition
Turned all to dust.
Only the well remains.
Once a source of life, now lonely amidst the stubble
Silent observer of destruction and death.

Whilst in the shadows of Lutyens' cathedral
The congregation of martial ghosts
Wander unnoticed by the pilgrim throng.

Without warning an errant breeze stirs the idle banners
The setting sun retires behind sullen clouds
Red bricks assume a duller guise
The moment fades and is gone.
Only the serried ranks of names are left
Etched in memories of stone.

A Soldier of the King

The bullets ploughed into his heaving breast
Knocking him to the sodden, frost-cold field.
As he fell he saw his father, Ghulam reaching out to him,
A look of pain and horror in his tearful eyes,
His name, Alam, upon his quivering lips.
He lay still, looking at the ashen sky, feeling no pain,
As if he had departed his shattered body;
He remembered the day the news had come,
Their King-Emperor across the black waters needed them,
He was in peril from the Hun hordes at his doorstep.
So like his father before him, a Sowar he became,
A proud member of Jacob's Horse.
Events tripped over each other in their urge to go,
Enlistment, tearful farewells, the long train trek
Until at Bombay the embarkation across October seas.
One sunny morn Marseilles was reached;
Another world of noise and colour; tumult and redolence
Where mysterious, pretty women, heads uncovered,
Eyed these dark-skinned men unashamedly

Gabbling unintelligible flatteries to them,
As they rode through the teeming streets to the station.
This was the last time he had seen the sun
So constant a presence, a companion of his previous life
Now the landscape grew darker, wetter, colder
Till their destination reached, Flanders in November,
Where ruins still held their strange-sounding names-
Festubert, Neuve-Chapelle and even Le Paradis!
Never had he been so cold, so homesick yet unafraid.
But he had his duty to the King-Emperor,
he depended on him;
So when the horses were taken
and infantry became their role,
It was a release from the boredom, it meant action,
Their first chance to show their worth, their courage.
Foot-slogging to Festubert, razed and ravaged.
A new year, but no new weather,
as they climbed from the trenches
A leaden January morning, drizzling sleet, a prayer to Allah,
Amidst the murderous machine-gun fire, he fell,
The stench of death already in the air, his fate sealed.
As the noise and chaos moved on, his father's face faded,
He was at the Jumma**, holding his mother's hand,
The mountains soaring above him, reaching up to Allah,
Strolling by the verdant fields his family
had tilled for generations –
The darkness crept over him, he smiled, content now
His duty done, he was a Soldier of the King-Emperor.

**Jumma- the fair in Bakra Bannu, North-West Frontier

A Soldier's a Man….his Life but a Span

Looking down from her view of the summer sea,
The sea that had carried him away from her love
All that was left, stored in the sanctity of a cardboard box,
Spread out on the ritually-scrubbed kitchen table –
A much-thumbed soldiers' Testament; a pencilled diary;
The dreaded War Office notification, form B104-82
Which had arrived in the same post as John's last missive
Followed a few days later by another letter containing
Detailed reference as to where he had been buried –
'1020 yards due east of rue de l'epinette, reference Festubert'.

With a sense of finality she picked up each remembrance,
Firstly the New Testament, studiously inscribed in ink
With his date of enlistment and the names of five friends
Who on that September day took the King's shilling with him.
Opening the diary, she read of menial tasks, days of boredom,
Fatigue and discomfort, even moments of humour
Punctuated by the exhilaration,
the naked terror of being under-fire.

The sun waned behind the headland as she came to the end,
Her eyes filled with tears realising for the first time
John's life in France had lasted a paltry forty-five days!

Picking up his last letter, she read again
of the dire wet weather;
'Hail falling the size of a shilling and getting washed out.
The rest of the day spent killing 'Grey Backs'
and washing clothes.'
Mundane words that meant everything, received
at the same time
As those heart-rending, portentous
'we regret to inform you...'
Dusk had now fallen, she drew the curtains, lit the lamps;
Returning to the table she picked up the
remaining remembrance
Her abiding hope, the key to release her pain,
assuage her grief –
When the war was over, a pilgrimage to her
soldier son's grave.
Determinedly, she gathered everything and
fastidiously returned it to the box.

*Remembering Private John M Paterson (2887) from Broxburn,
Linlithgowshire, 7th. (Fife) Battalion, the Black Watch (Royal
Highlanders) killed in action on June 15th. 1915. As in so
many cases, grave location detail was wasted. She would never
see her beloved son's grave; the war passed on, returned and
obliterated every trace and today he is commemorated on Le
Touret Memorial to the Missing, not far from where he fell.*

A Trickle of Sand

He trickled the fine, warm sand through his fingers,
As the heat pressed down on his carefully covered head
His eyes squinting into the relentless, interrogating sun,
Images and haze combining to imagine
A vigilant foe behind every palm tree, every dune.

It was the second day of watching the emotionless desert;
A forward observation post to warn of attack,
His first responsibility since he accepted the stripes.
Reluctant to take the promotion and 'lose his mates,'
But once the decision had been made and accepted,
He mused, he was determined to do it right.
He trickled the fine, warm sand through his fingers.

His patrol was a mixed bunch, mainly lowland Scots,
Untried in battle, awed by everything they saw,
But he 'thought they'd do, indeed 'hoped they'd do!'
If not, he believed it was up to him to ensure they did.
His judgment was always to see the best in people,
Instilled in him by his parents and life in the manse.

Settling down as dusk approached, watchful and wary,
Ensuring sentries were posted, vigilant and alert,
He trickled the fine, warm sand through his hands,
Before writing the letter home as he regularly did.

On a misty, sullen day in late April
A solitary cyclist delivered the fateful telegram

To the lonely manse at the head of the glen,
Followed three days later by a scribbled anonymous note
Posted in Egypt to avoid the censor's pen.

A confession of guilt, from a so-called 'comrade,'
The lonely post attacked just after dusk by an insatiable foe,
All turned and fled into the desert to safety,
Leaving Archie, to face death heroically, but alone.
No-one knew the truth, but it preyed on his craven mind,
Ending cryptically, 'I could say much more.'
The pain of their loss was tempered by the knowledge of duty,
He died true to his beliefs, a reflection of their upbringing.

Then the solitary cyclist returned again to enhance their grief,
His broken body found still facing forward at his post
Archie's last letter, miraculously salvaged
from the unfeeling desert,
Opened at the heart of the home where he had said
his last farewell;
Unfolded with a gasp of shock at the unexpected
proximity to their son,
A trickle of fine sand upon the kitchen table.

A true story. In memory of Corporal Archibald Taylor
ALEXANDER 7611

1st/5th Bn.-Royal Scots Fusiliers——23/04/1916 Age 21 of
Irvine, Ayrshire—KANTARA WAR MEMORIAL CEMETERY-
F. 220

Angel Worship

From the scream of battle
He was manhandled with care
To a place where hope glimmered
But death still desired and often won.
Into this chaos of blood, stink and gore
She stepped, cool serenity.

Uniform starched, but softness in the eyes
Disciplined care, nay almost love
Slowly brought back life, health again
And time too for him to stare, to worship.

Closer meditation saw beneath
The untouchable angel-veneer –
This naïve dispassionate observer of naked maleness
But never for her alone.

A blooming young beauty;
Hiding her youth, her girlish giggles
Behind the austerity of uniform –
Closed doors of necessary propriety –
One day to be freed, gladly shared –
But for now alone his unobtainable icon
Worshipped for the hint of errant hair;
A sensual psalm to faraway eyes.

Authuille on a Summer's Eve – Musings

Nine o'clock at night after a scorching day;
The sun reluctantly retreats behind the skyline,
Across the valley Aveluy Wood bathed in soft, hazy sunlight,
A desultory train meanders along the valley;
The church clock lazy chimes the hour,
A cooling breeze rustles the restless trees.

Along the alley comes the smell of a well-done barbeque;
The sound of the important business of opening – tin and
bottle,Gallic conversation, gentle, persuasive
and pleasant to the ear.
By the lane to Lonsdale Cemetery the ever-present ducks,
Regale each other with yet another joke; the
old ones are the best,
While framed in the shed window, his overnight home,
The family hound listens ears cocked but uncomprehending
Mutt that he is failing to appreciate the
subtleties of canard humour,
He flops down dreaming of being let loose in the duck pen.

1 3

The road up the hill next to the wood leads to Mesnil.
Memories of home and family and Bonfire Night
Inspired the ever inventive, but homesick Tommy
to call it Brock's Benefit,
After the well-known firework manufacturer.
To ascend the hill you meander past the church;
Past the war memorial; a fairly standard issue model,
Head and shoulders of an armless poilu on a plinth
Above immortal names of those who marched away,
Dying for Mother France on some distant field.

A Desailly is there, lost amongst the many;
I wonder if he had the family face, peasant, but warm,
open, trustworthy?
The village flowers beneath the Fallen are
the Mayor's responsibility
A stolid, square citizen, a perpetual Gaulois cemented
to his bottom lip,
More at home in shorts perfecting the lines of potatoes
beneath our home,
Than in his suit and Republican sash on days of note.
Phlegmatic, unfazed, a man of the soil, I like him.

The road abruptly descends to the bridge across the Ancre,
Beloved by Blunden, a friendly, happy little river,
But not before passing our beloved and
much frequented Auberge,
Silent tonight, it's Monday, but the lure of Bourgogne magic
still lingers here.
Opposite a small neat house, once the home of
a big man in every sense,
Now gone to be larger than death in Walloon Valhalla,
never to be forgotten.

The sun has gone now and I need mentally
meander no further tonight,

Where better to end this flight of fancy, than beside the Ancre,
Where once comradeship meant more than life itself?
The sound of the river and thoughts of two dear friends,
One stilled forever, but eternally in our thoughts;
The other also larger than life, a terrible man,
Self-styled 'serial killer' and chef extraordinaire.
A perfect pair of bookends!

*Dedie aux les deux "serre-livres" – DENIS BOURGOGNE ,
Chef Extraordinaire et ETIENNE BEKAERT , deux homes
plus grands dans tous les sens , les deux chers amis. Et aussi
JEAN-CLAUDE DESAILLY dans l'amitié et pour sa gentil-
lesse*

Authuille – un soir à l'approche de l'été – Reflections

Neuf heures du soir après une journée chaude
et bien ensoleillée
Le soleil se cache derrière l'horizon.
De l 'autre côté de la vallée, le bois d'Aveluy se jouit
de ce temps doux
Un train se dirige le long de la vallée
Le clocher de l'église sonne l'heure
Un petit coup de vent dérange les feuilles des arbres

Un odeur agréable de bbq pénètre dans l'allée
Et on entend ceux qui s'occupent aux choses
sérieuses – overture
des boites et des bouteilles
Une conversation, douce et persuasive se fait entendre,
agréable à l'oreille.
Sur le petit chemin qui mène au cimetière de Lonsdale,
les chansons de canards
se font comme chaque jour – ils échangent leurs
sentiments et plaisenteries du jour,
Les vieilles sont toujours les meilleurs.
Encadré dans son niche, le chien de
meute passe la nuit
Il écoute, les oreilles pointées en haut,
mais il ne comprend pas les badinages
des canards et il se recouche et rêve que l'on
le laisse chasser ces bêtes

La petite route monte la colline qui mène à Mesnil
Les souvenirs d'être chez soi avec la famille et on se
rappelle de ce qui
S'est passé il y a longtemps le 5 novembre
Le Tommy, ayant mal à son pays s'inspire et renomme cet
endroit « Brock's Benefit »
Après le fabricant d'artifices bien connu

Pour monter la pente, vous passez l'église,
puis le Mémorial (un peu ordinaire),
Une statue de tête et épaule d'un poilu sur une plinthe,
Au dessous sont gravés les noms de ceux qui sont partis
Et ont trouvé la mort, loin de chez eux pour
l'honneur de la France

Un Desailly s'y trouve mais perdu dans la longue liste
Je me demande s'il avait le visage familial,
fils de la terre mais chaleureux,
ouvert et de bonne foi ?
Les fleurs au dessus du mémorial aux morts sont
à la responsabilité du M. le Maire.,
Un citoyen solide, grand et carré, la gauloise perpétuelle dans
la bouche et collée à sa lèvre inférieure – plus à l'aise dans son
short à s'occuper des sillons droits des
rangées de pommes de terre que dans sa costume
de devoir et son écharpe
républicaine pour les obligations de son métier.
Phlegmatique, sans soucis,
un homme de la terre, je l'aime.

Maintenant la route descend vers le
pont pour franchir l'Ancre
Aimé par Blunden, ces eaux lui plaisaient beaucoup
Mais avant de traverser le pont,
nous passons devant notre restaurant,
Très aimé et souvent visité.

Ce soir, tout est calme car c'est lundi mais la magie
Bourgogne se attarde toujours là
En face, une petite maison, anciennement habitée par un
grand homme, grand dans tous les sens – maintenant même
plus grand que la mort dans la Valhalla de
Walloon. On se souviendra de lui.

Le soleil s'est couché, je n'ai plus besoin de réflêchir ce soir,
Il n'y a pas de meilleur endroit que de se trouver
sur les rives de l'Ancre
Où, il y a longtemps, la camaraderie comptait
autant que la vie elle-même
Le petit bruit des eaux nous fait penser à nos deux chers amis,
L'un, dont la voix est disparu mais qui sera
éternellement dans nos pensées.
L'autre, aussi grande en stature, un homme terrible
Connu comme « serial killer » et chef extraordinaire
Une paire parfaite de « serre-livres »

*Dedie aux les deux "serre-livres" – DENIS BOURGOGNE ,
Chef Extraordinaire et ETIENNE BEKAERT , deux homes
plus grands dans tous les sens , les deux chers amis. Et
aussi JEAN-CLAUDE DESAILLY dans l'amitié et pour sa
gentillesse*

Big Brother

To 2Lt. C A R (Bunny) Tennant of Orford House, Ugley, Essex,
killed in action 1915 aged 26

The apple trees were old and gnarled,
But still gave grubby fruit and dappled shade;
She sat beneath the one they played in,
The faded photo clenched in arthritic fingers;
He looked so old in his pristine uniform,
She so little and doll-like in her Sunday dress.
The next day he was gone.
The letters came so full of fun
He could have been at school
No hint of fear, of mud, of death
Then they stopped.
Bemused she pestered mother,
Until the day the telegram came;
Then hysteria filled the air,
Mother sobbing solitary in her room;
Ashen-faced father, no time to explain

To love, to wrap in loving arms.
He had only been her brother
Not a grown-up, just twelve years older
But she let him hold her hand,
Give her scrumped apples, always the best ones,
Bathe cuts and bruises,
Carry her on shoulders in the blossom above her world;
She even did as she was told!
Big brother.
So long ago yet as yesterday.
Her hand relaxed, he would come soon,
The sepia memory fluttered gently to the ground.
When they found her, a smile upon her lips
An unblemished apple had fallen in her lap.

By any Other Name....

Napoleon's citizen army
Rustic, rural, agricultural.
Nivelle's lambs to the slaughter
Baa-ing like sheep as they attacked.
Grumblers all, 'grognards,'
Or the Hairy ones –
Poilus

Antipodean miners in the Boer War
Egalitarian and enduring.
Anzac Cove, dig for your lives;
Mates dying together.
Nothing more important
Than your cobber –
Diggers

Ottoman army;
Anatolian gun fodder;
Stubborn, brave, obedient.

Foot soldiers
Delivering their motherland.
Lacking equipment, not guts
Prepared to die –
Mehmetcik

Yankees covered in dust
Adobes or cooking?
American-Mexico war.
Expeditionary force,
'Kill the Hun' roars Black Jack.
Arrogant, cocky, naïve –
Doughboys

Eighteenth century Flanders
Boxtel battlefield.
Name? asks the Iron Duke.
Satisfied, inspired
It sticks – 1914 deja vu
Summoned at Christmas –
Tommy Atkins

Christmas Day 1917

In the nether land twixt slumber and waking,
He was aware of the murmur of foreign laughter;
Opening his eyes he saw the white-coated doctor
Deep in conversation with the uniformed nurses –
A spasm of naked pain wracked his whole frame,
Crying out involuntarily they ceased and turned to look.
One approached uttering meaningless,
                yet comforting words
As he wiped his fevered brow.

He remembered, the bullet had hit him
As he clambered awkwardly from the safety of the trench,
Burying itself deep within his stomach.
When he awoke, the dusk had fallen,
Overwhelmed by searing pain, he cried out
                'Mother, help me.'
As if she had heard his plea, from the encroaching gloom,
Two spectres appeared, manhandling him onto a stretcher.
Then began a journey through the barriers of pain
To this field-hospital set up in a ruined stable,
                where he lay.

The orderly arose, shrugging his shoulders;
The doctor wrote lazily and hastily left.
Alone, the insidious pain held sway,
Even the feverish memories of home and family
Were at the remote corners of his agitated mind
As he slowly slipped away.

Later the nurse returned, held his wrist and without emotion
Pulled the regulation blanket over his tormented face.
In the corner the Christmas Tree shimmered brightly
Outside the snowy scene scintillated by the eastern star
Echoed to the strains of 'Heilige Nacht, Stille Nacht.'

*In memory of Rowland Faircloth who lived in my road and
died a prisoner-of-war on Christmas Day*

Christmas 'W' Beach 1915

It was all over now; it was time to leave.
So many left behind, Constantinople
a faded dream.
Midnight saw us at W Beach just before Christmas.
A time of peace, of brotherly love,
But of necessity, a time to keep low, the head down,
To avoid the sniper's ever-vigilant eye –
We would soon be departing for good,
Not as thieves in the night, but as soldiers,
Our memories raw, our farewells exhausted.

Christmas Eve, one lifetime ago,
too many beers in 'The Plough,'
Snoring in the midnight pew with Walter,
So long ago even Walter's cheeky grin had faded;
A Turkish delight broke the calm of
the present peaceful day,
Four nonchalant planes scattering gifts from above
On waiting supplicants, leaving festive red upon the sand
Captain Cox, the only officer left from the April landing,
A direct hit, his good fortune ended.

Christmas Day, Johnny Turk was quiet,
perhaps he knew?
But the hostile sea was short on understanding
Few supplies were landed, but there were plum puddings,
Bully beef made tasty rissoles,
and officers joked with other ranks

Not like home, of course, but the dug-outs
exuded good cheer
And ghostly friends watched and approved,
A window of earthly peace and goodwill
Engraved forever into their candid souls,
With their fallen comrades, never to be forgotten.

Coincidence

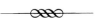

As the pain hit him he fell; the rifle flew from his grasp
Landing in the noxious mud swallowing it up
But cushioning him as he followed its downward path.
He lay, the warm blood trickling down his neck
Under his sweat-soaked tunic and he smiled content.
Blighty beckoned, the nightmare was over;
His lost rifle symbolic of a new future.

Inanimate, forgotten among the detritus of war
The rifle waited as the mud took its toll
Rotting the wooden stock, insinuating rust
Even a trundling tank bending the arrow-straight barrel.
Condemned to the depths of a Flanders' field,
Awaiting discovery, rescue from its primeval shroud
To be harvested and renewed.

Time passed, the day came, inquisitive probing,
By man and machine, unearthed, excavated, cleansed.
Easy pickings, so many to find, but what were their stories?

Did they curtail someone's existence
Or had they never been used in anger?
Amidst the mystery, coincidence, one hundred years later
A British rifle chosen randomly amongst many
Property of one careful owner wounded, discharged unfit.

Cricket on a Summer's Day

The summer heat insisted he close his eyes –
In his mind's eye he could see the village green,
smell the cut grass;
The heavy roller protesting the interruption
of its weekly slumber
On its perambulation up and down the pitch
of dew-fresh carpet.
But opening his heavy lids, the knowledge of where he dozed
Was all too harsh, heat haze over the lake,
desultory trees, hills behind.

Returning to the preferable reverie on home and cricket –
His first match; donning heavy pads with begloved fingers,
Murmurs of good luck, laughter about forgetting the box;
Bertha could help him there, until red-faced, eager
Out down the steps, polite applause,
to face the sweating bowler
Brawny, broad of girth, the blacksmith
and ever-ready pugilist.

Memory of the first innings was as brief
as his stay in the middle;
Clatter of stumps, then the long walk back in deadly silence;
Bertha's blue dress; wishing the ground
would swallow him up.
Arrogance had been his undoing, ignominious his departure
Then he was gone, bucolic Essex an ever-fading dream
Until the scorching plains of Suvla became his arena.

The present reality would brook no further impediment –
All that mattered was this moment, the attack,
but insidious memories
Still would not leave as he instinctively
adjusted his equipment
Wryly musing that a box would be useful now!
It was a matter of honour, he would not fail again
Holding bat aloft he rose out the trench towards
the waiting fielders.

A ripple of gunfire as he strode purposely towards the middle
Feeling all eyes upon him, even Bertha was
there urging him on.
Taking guard, middle and leg, all seemed still,
the watchers tense
He surveyed the field. Nothing different there
He was ready, calm, determined awaiting the demon
bowler's approach
He was confident it would be short, and as it pitched
darkness descended.

Dawn July 1st 1916

⸺❈⸺

Just another summer day with the promise
of warmth and blue skies.
The sun already colouring and warming the eastern sky.
The gentle breeze caressing the ancient trees
in the nearby wood.
A dawn chorus with a solo blackbird taking centre stage
Bursting his lungs with delight at another dawn,
Peace on earth, another summer's day in Picardie.
But scratch the surface of this template for the perfect dawn
In subterranean dugouts and a labyrinth of trenches
A myriad of men waiting for their destiny to unfold
Witnessing the birth of their last day on earth
Before an unsuspecting rendezvous with death.
A wisp of smoke; an inaudible murmur; a nervous cough
The crisp click as polished bayonets are fixed.
The prelude to a day after which the old world would vanish;
When a volunteer citizen army would evanesce in glory;
When innocence would die in a storm of machine-gun bullets.

Written at 6.45 a.m. on the Somme on July 1st 2014

Deborah

From the haven of his hospital bed
From under crisp white linen
Face bandaged like a shroud
He penned his letter about Deborah –
No estaminet floosie this Deborah, but a tank
Knowing full-well no-one would understand.
It was impossible to equate name with object
But he tried, a thin smile upon his lips as he toiled
It was always his lot, his destiny even
His wayward father had run off with the postmistress
Rubenesque, who liked her stamps licked!
Leaving bitter mother, five sisters and him.
Despite this he knew nothing about women – who did?
He liked them, but a female tank was another matter.

For six months he had shared the metal womb
Cramped with seven others, deafened by the noise
Nauseous from the fumes and when bullets hit outside
His young face, bloody and scarred from

Hot metal splinters ricocheting inside.
Rumbling along, three measly miles an hour
Clad in iron, seemingly invincible
The new Excalibur.

It had been a misty day in November as they crept
Ponderously towards the fearsome Hindenberg Line
No obstacle could brook their triumph it seemed
The Hun fled in panic, victory was in their sights
But from the jaws of victory, defeat was grasped
Over-cautious, reticent, the attack faltered and all was lost.
For Deborah, near Flesquieres five direct hits
Aborted their progress, disembowelling midships
Leaving carnage and mutilation.
For him the sanctuary of unconsciousness, saved him –
The nightmares bad enough without the blood-spattered
Memories of the five others to haunt him.
The shell-torn earth received them, comrades forever
Beneath the white sentinels of remembrance.
For Deborah an anonymous hole.

Time passed, memories faded
Only an old lady hazily remembered where she lay –
A precocious child nosily watching as she disappeared
Into the primeval mud of a wet winter's day
Forgotten until a resurrection beckoned
The elderly memory creaked a little, informed help needed
But Deborah was found and the old lady was content.
Today she stands a tribute to the bravery of men;
The perseverance of the pioneer pursuing a dream
Rescued from the anonymity of another time
Where unsurprisingly she has the last word!

Inspired by a visit to see 'Deborah,' a Mark IV female tank.

Dedication of the War Memorial
April 7th 1921

The April sun shone weakly over the assembled throng
As he found a secluded spot above the scene.
That morning for the first time since they came,
He had, with trembling hands, opened the box of medals.
It had been difficult to assemble the gaudy ribbons,
But he persevered, awkwardly pinning them
on with safety pins.

Making his way laboriously, leaning heavily on his stick,
He found his place by the Baptist Church,
Looking down the High Street over the hushed throng
Resplendent in their Sunday best,
a sea of fluttering Union flags.
Remembrance and pride had been the order of the day,
Not grief, but the numbers of spotless white handkerchiefs
And the sound of smothered sobs, belied this.

It was nearly three years since the guns fell silent;
Five since a Hun bullet had shattered his ankle –
and his dreams.
But although he awoke less, sweating and afraid
And the faces had begun to fade, he remembered
With frightening clarity how each of them went –
Walter, at Suvla, carelessly standing up in the trench,
Shot in the head , whilst extolling the virtues
of the buxom Bertha
Whom he loved. Sid, ever eager, the first over the top at Serre,
The first to be killed and Tom, near the end, near Achiet,
Hit by the creeping barrage and never seen again, not a trace.

The dedication done, the afternoon sun slid
behind the watching houses;
On the skyline witness through the ages, the ancient church
Now saw the slow dispersal of the still hushed crowd
Slow as they lingered over beloved names; reluctant to leave,
to finalise their loss.
He waited, till all but a few remained, making his way
Through the assembled riot of poppies,
up the steps to the names.
Names of school-friends, comrades,
nearly overwhelming him,
So many, so long ago, it seemed.

He turned, his first intent to go down the hill to
the Comrades Club,
But even the prospect of a beer did not attract him –
He wanted, no, needed to be alone with his memories.
Once home he carefully removed the medals replacing them
in their boxes.
Sitting by the fire, he wept for the first time,
Sobs that wracked his slender frame, tears for friends,
for the loss of innocence,
For himself – till he could weep no more and he slept.

Deep and Crisp and Even

A multitude of horrors lay under the cocoon of snow.
It had started as the winter day limped to its frigid finale,
Gently at first, then smothering flakes like cotton wool,
Slowly masking the dead Boche, an abomination,
Who, for days before, lay festering in No Man's Land,
Till his awfulness softly disappeared into
a recumbent snow figure.
The pale moon gently filtered its aura over the scene
Reminding the watchers of dream-like times at home
Light years away; a timeless vista of peace and calm.
Transfixed by this day-dream of another existence,
An errant whizz-bang rudely violated this innocent reverie
Blowing the snow-shrouded somnambulant
Hun to smithereens
Coating the virgin snow with crimson, festive gore,
Relegating the remembered cherished other world
To the stark horrors of another day in hell.
'Stand To!'

Eggs or Surrender

'The Major wants some eggs, Joe,' shaking
him on the shoulder.
Joe stirred and looked uncomprehendingly at Fred,
Blinking in the early morning sunlight
he suddenly remembered.
He was not at home with his beloved Eliza gently snoring
next to him.
Running his fingers though his tousled hair
He gazed upon the Holy City resplendent before them
Jerusalem – he remembered Sundays at St Peter's,
How he hated the forced attendance to 'improve his soul,'
But there had been the charms of Eliza to look at
Besides Mother had sent him, and when Mother told you….

'Joe, wake up you lazy bugger, the Major
wants his breakfast!'
Reverie over he stood up, stretched and pulled on his tunic,
The calm of the crisp winter's dawning,
After the noise of conflict was succour to his ears,
This quiet was interrupted by Fred's Cockney interjection,
'Where are we going to find eggs, Joe?'
It was a pointless query, they both knew it,
Having been in the Army long enough,
an order was an order,
The Major would brook no failure, he was
not a man to upset,
So find eggs it was, no room for negotiation or error.

The birds heralded their stroll through the broken streets,
Past shattered buildings from where dark eyes
Curiously assessed their latest conquerors,
Pedestrian crusaders with their strange
accents and ready smiles.
There was no sign of eggs, nor likely to be,
But the sun shone, their accompanying chorus continued
As they ventured casually towards the Christian Mecca.

Suddenly in the near distance an ominous group appeared,
Joe unhooked his rifle, took the safety catch off, "Look out!"
Then he caught sight of a grubby white flag held aloft
By one amongst the be-suited group.
Not a weapon in sight, deferentially, slowing their pace
The gap between them merged until face-to-face.

Awkward silence broken only by the chorister birds.
'Look that fella's got a camera,' chirped up Fred,
There he was grinning widely, clicking away.
'Effendi,' the words broke the silence,
'This is Hussein Effendi El-Hussein the mayor,
the mayor of Jerusalem,
He greets you, and offers you the city of David.'
Joe surveyed the grey-haired man in the fez
Holding out his supplicant hands towards them,
Before he could speak, Fred, in embarrassment blurted out,
'Have you got any eggs, Guv?'

Bemused the mayor turned and whispered to his aide
Who almost imploringly repeated, 'We surrender the city!'
In a sudden movement, Fred with a nod
that was almost a bow
Grasped the outstretched hands, saluted and
with a muttered 'Come on,'
Turned abruptly and quick-marched back
the way they had come.

The puzzled group shrugged their shoulders
and retraced their steps

Major Barry was impatiently waiting for them, barking out
'Where are my eggs?' 'Couldn't find any, sir,' responded Fred.
The Major was not pleased, 'and why not?'
'Met the mayor, sir, he wanted to surrender the city instead.'
'Damn the surrender, I want my eggs, sergeant.'
He uncharacteristically sighed, 'Contact HQ and tell them.'
And with a grumpy salute he disappeared into his tent.
The two sergeants saluted, looked at one another,
Shrugged their shoulders and headed to the radio tent,
'Close shave that, said Joe, 'the Major must
be in a good mood....'

*On the 9th December 1917 the Mayor of Jerusalem Hussein
Effendi El-Hussein accompanied by his aids and soldiers of the
Ottoman Empire, made a white flag and went out in search of
the British forces' front line in order to surrender. They even
brought a camera crew along to record the event. They came
across two British Sergeants from the 60th London Division
(artillery, reconnaissance duty) on the outskirts of Jerusalem.
The two sergeants had left camp in order to search for some-
thing for their officer's breakfast – the officer being Major F.R
Barry. The mayor of Jerusalem attempted to surrender to
Sergeants F. G. Hurcomb & J. Sedgwick. They were however
more interested in knowing where they could obtain some eggs
and tea for their officer's breakfast.*

*The Mayor made at least two further attempts to surrender
the city before he succeeded!*

Encore Plus Que La Vie
(More than Life Itself)

She felt better as she breathed in the fresh, salty air,
It was six days into the voyage and home grew ever nearer.
She had left the two girls playing in the cabin;
She needed to clear her head, subdue
the nausea in her stomach;
The same ever-present sickness that persuaded
her to return home for a while.
After five years she longed for the smell of
heather, not for good,
Just till the interminable discomfort eased,
when Daniel would follow.
Leaving had been painful, the girls
sobbing uncontrollably;
She busily fussing to hold back her tears;
Daniel tight-lipped, a contrived smile to mask his grief.
Her thoughts were shattered as from the corner of her eye
She saw the torpedo hit mid-ships and a huge explosion.
Knocked off her feet, the deck seemed to keel over.
Screaming, helpless, she slid towards the oily depths;
In eighteen minutes the mighty ship had gone.

At home in Washington Daniel submerged
his emptiness in work.
They had decided he should stay; their new life
too good to lose.
Hopefully home would ease Mary's condition.

Waving goodbye, as the figures on deck faded
into the distance,
Worried until they had crossed the perilous ocean.
Neutral though America ostensibly was,
He did not trust the actions of the Hun – remember Belgium!
When the news came it was a sledgehammer
of pain – all gone!
There was no room for mourning, only the
outlet of naked rage.
There was nothing worth living for ever again
Revenge obsessed his desolate soul;
There was only one course left, to return, to enlist, to die.

It was chill in the trench as the Spring day dawned
The early-rising birds greeted a new day with hope and song
But for Daniel another day only meant
a day nearer to release.
Scotland offered no haven from his nightmares
There was too much to remind him; too much sympathy
The Thin Red Line absorbed him, asked no questions.
He prospered as a soldier, fearless, nonchalant with danger
Ever striving to be with them once again.
In his hand he held a much-handled crumpled photograph
Suddenly he turned to his sole friend who knew,
'I shall see Mary and the bairns today,' he said,
with a broad smile
And continued with even more fervour polishing his bayonet.

The whistle blew and he scrambled out of the trench,
From Beaucamp an incessant stream of bullets rent the air,
Men fell everywhere but it was as if his life was charmed –
There suddenly in front of him he could see
the girls and Mary.
On and on he ran, stretching out his hand towards them,
Chest heaving calling out their names until
a shell burst near him;

Hot, jagged shrapnel tore into his chest and he fell.
When they found him, lying amidst a field of wild flowers
He seemed to be embracing something within his grasp,
Turning him over he looked serene, fulfilled, content,
A smile of pure joy upon his ingenuous face.

In Memory of the Lambie family –

Mrs Mary Lambie, wife of Daniel Lambie, with her two daughters, aged 9 & 6 yrs, embarked on the Lusitania for Liverpool. None of them ever reached port. On learning that his wife and two children had gone down with the ship, Lambie, enlisted and died with 14th Argyll and Sutherland Highlanders on 24th. April 1917

Etaples

With a squealing, and hissing the train ground to a halt
Awakening her with surprise from her reverie –
A distant daydream of a summer's day on the river
The day he had first caught her in his arms and kissed her.
Then all was still and the birds sang amidst the rolling dunes
The passengers were all standing,
the men had doffed their caps.
Looking through the window she realized why
Before them stretched a sea of silent sentinels
Stretching away in military order to the cross on the hill.
The huge immediacy of the cemetery,
The realization that he was there, that this was
the end of her pilgrimage
Momentarily un-nerved her and she sat down,
hiding the tears.
Behind her veil of mourning with gratifying success
No-one seemed to notice, politely avoiding her eyes.
With a squealing and hissing the train
awoke and moved on.

It had been a long journey from her poky bed-sit in Clapham,
But a necessity, a promise to herself fulfilled;
A pledge made when the letter from the chaplain arrived
Shattering her future, laying waste her present,
Despoiling her innocence, embellishing her past.
It had been his first leave since their marriage
A short time of intense, surreal passion
And then he had gone, leaving her a solitary figure
Waving, waving until the asthmatic train
Had turned the corner and left the
world and Waterloo empty.

Now three empty, heart-broken years later
The beckoning promise troubled her no more.
She could now say goodbye, could lay to rest her love.
The garrulous, Gaullois-smoking taxi-driver
Ever appreciative of a pretty face, a well-turned ankle
Was struck by her pale beauty that no veil could mask,
Shook his head sadly and cursed the Boche
For causing such undeserved pain,
He, too, had lost an only son on the Chemin-des-Dames,
His beloved Angelique had faded away soon after.
He wanted to comfort her, say the right words,
She acknowledged his awkward sympathy with a faint smile,
Her mind elsewhere.

It was a late summer's afternoon, the sun reflecting on the bay
When she overlooked the interminable rows of white
headstones
So many she panicked, she would never find him
But the comfort of the letter with his location marked
Calmed her as she slowly descended the stone steps.
Once down, she followed the winding rows of officers' graves
Momentarily wondering if this was where the King,
In an act of regal poignancy, had left the violets,
Until she stopped and there he was....

As the brilliant orb of sun slipped over the horizon,
A chill breeze from the estuary caused her to shiver,
The endless tears upon her pale cheeks had at
last ceased and dried;
In the near distance she became aware that
With a muted squealing, and hissing
Another obeisant train had ground to a halt.

Fifteen Paces. . . . .Pause

Fifteen paces, pause. Fifteen paces, pause.
Alf was a well-known sight with his trusty hound.
Every day without fail he shuffled from his home
Up the High Street to collect his paper
Dressed always in his Hospital Blues
Carrying his money in his hand, no pockets in blues!
A gas-shell had destroyed his lungs on the Somme.
Returning home a crippled shadow of a former self
Wheezing heroically wearing his blue badge of courage –
No white feathers for him.
Determined nothing the Kaiser had thrown at him would stop
his daily routine –
Till one day he was gone.
Death's inexorable progress had stilled his plucky spirit;
His neatly folded blues, a rag and bone man's
unexpected treasure.
But not quite gone without trace –
His dog remained, forgotten, lonely, a burden,
Till one day suddenly noticed,

A son was detailed to exercise 'that bloody dog' –
Reluctant and complaining he ventured forth
Only to return vehemently declaring,
'That's the last time I take that dog, all it does is,
Fifteen paces, pause. Fifteen paces, pause.'

Somewhere Alf smiled a knowing smile,

Following Helen

Oh Hell of ships and cities,
Hell of men like me,
Fatal second Helen,
Why must I follow thee

The great Trojan adventure re-visited.
Warriors in khaki, sans shields, sans spears;
Educationally familiar with place,
Set sail with a cast of thousands
As if it had always been their destiny
Not just a scholarly exercise seducing many.

Prepared to die, but not willing to submit
Better to stand in a trench and evoke the Gods
Gods whose purpose was to encourage,
cajole, demand
That as warriors death became a necessity.

The great Trojan adventure ended in failure and death.
The latter-day Spartans embittered
Disillusioned, leaving behind the human vestiges of defeat
For the killing fields of France.

Perhaps it was the need to re-invent himself
Appalled at the abject failure, guilty for those who fell
He, double-barrelled of name, romantic of spirit
Forsook the spoiled Classics and took refuge
in the ancient sagas;

Norse-like he grew a beard –
A beard that shouted defiance, imbued martial anger
Because it was red – profane, shocking and red!

Thus double-barrelled, red-bearded, our warrior
Determined on his path to Valhalla –
Equipped, ready for death, undefeated –
Patrick Shaw-Stewart, unshaven, fiery and magnificent.

*Remembering Lieut-Commander PATRICK HOUSTON
SHAW-STEWART Hood Bn. R.N. Div Royal Naval Volunteer
Reserve kia 30/12/1917 aged 29*

*Chevalier of the Legion of Honour. Croix De Guerre
(France). Son of Maj. Gen. John Heron Maxwell Shaw Stewart
and Mary Catherine Bedingfeld Shaw Stewart. A poet,
Shaw-Stewart was educated at Eton and Balliol College,
Oxford. Hertford and Ireland Scholarships; Double First. He
was considered by his peers to be brilliant. He fought at
Gallipoli and on his return to France grew a beard which was
unexpectedly red! He was later killed and is buried in METZ-
EN-COUTURE COMMUNAL CEMETERY BRITISH
EXTENSION-II. E. 1*

Fragment....

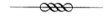

Finding the fractured femur
At the edge of a fallow field
It felt right that we should 'fossick' for more.
Frenetically we followed each furrow
Before the fusilade of rain threatened all.
Finally we felt we had found enough,
Enough for a full-scale funeral'
Fantastically among the foraged findings
A fractured fusilier badge fulfilled
A finality.

Fragments from Fromelles

Cold fields awaiting enervating plough;
Old bones fallow, rotting anonymously;
Forgotten as last year's crops,
Suddenly stirred, re-awakened by the threat of intrusive iron.
A shaft of sunlight; a simultaneous stirring of memory;
A link to the future, a bond with the past,
A longing to answer, to reveal the loss.
Questions unanswered, the need to identify,
To open the secrets of the dead, men who obeyed,
Whose comrades were all; the poultice of remembrance.
Unforgotten, engulfed in memory, in lore, in love.
The regret to be exorcised; the pride to be shared:
Semblance of an answer, a marker to worship:
A debt to be paid.

'Friendly Fire!'

One last letter to write, the most difficult lie yet,
The horror still fresh in everyone's minds
Too many witnesses to tell the truth,
what would be gained
The innocent culprit was distraught, eager to die,
A wish likely to be fulfilled on the morrow for them all.

Tomorrow, out over the top and then Berlin... perhaps.
It had happened here in Railway Hollow
Behind the reassuringly named Evangelist Copses
Where the little railway came.

Atkins, not yet eighteen, from the back-to-back streets of
Accrington
Thin as a rake, eager to please, proud of being a Pal
The first time in his life belonging,
having friends, having regular grub;
Cleaning his rifle with naïve vigour so it shone
like no other, so it was the best.

His little idyll carelessly rent by the fateful retort;
his dreams shattered
By his side two pals dead, Tom through the head,
Bob the chest.
Witnessed by all, the blood on the grass,
the nightmare real.
Young Atkins hysterically distraught,
a soldier no more.

Tough by name, not by nature,
the captain chewed his pencil
It was no use writing to those left at home,
Regaling them with the bitter truth – to what end?
Better to write those three over-used words
'killed in action' – pain enough.

Everyone shared the lie, complicit in a sensitive silence;
The memory ingrained deep in their souls forever;
Remembered but never spoken of again –
it was easier that way
For Atkins, death seemed the only salvation and
it failed him not.

As they marched under the chestnut trees by the
Sucrerie next day,
Surveying sweating sappers digging a large hole,
'Escaping to Orstralia?' a wag called from the
curious passers-by,
'No mate, it's for you lot!' stilling abruptly the ripple of
mirth. – and it was!

Today they rest in the finite comradeship of death –
Bob and Tom lie next to one another,
their secret shared ,
Shared but never spoken of,
even by those who came back.

Nearby their captain lies, the pencil chewed no more,
the lie complete,
Even Atkins lies content somewhere in those rolling fields
His penance done, a Pal once more.

Based on a true event.

Ghosts Tread Softly

Through the timeless mists of a summer morning
Breaks the wailing of an ancient call to arms
Intrusive shots awake the nesting birds and rabbits flee,
From the safe womb of trenches clamber the khaki figures
The sleeping earth suddenly rent by missiles of death
Recumbent figures caress the mother earth
And compliant Death opens his welcoming arms.
Today the larks still sing; the fields drowse unmoved
But ghosts tread softly on the corn and in our memory.

JULY 1ST 2012

Grandad's Great War

I

It was an impulse that drew him into the seedy building.
Every day he had walked past the
long queues of young men
Chattering with excitement as the unknown
adventure of war beckoned.
Perhaps it was a momentary hiatus at the
perceived onset of old age;
A desire to keep a grasp on youth as long as he could,
But surprising even himself he joined the eager throng.

'Are you sure, sir' the RSM queried, paternally,
'You are thirty-seven with a missus,
and two young 'uns!
Why not wait, the call will come soon for everyone.'
But, no, he insisted, his call had come,
so the deed was done.

Walking briskly home, his ardour gradually faded,
his steps got slower.
Proud, defiant, yet nervous he entered
the house and sat down,
The small-talk of the day's events
unfolded until he could stand no more
Suddenly blurting out, 'I've joined up!'-
Silence, then tears flowed, anger at his irresponsibility.
Finally a resignation and perhaps a tinge of pride.

II

Easter Monday, Arras 1917 huddling into
any draught-free corner,
Beneath the derelict city dusted with snow
waiting for zero-hour.
He pondered, thinking of the home he had
left on a patriotic whim.
He had coped with the dirt, the squalor, the fear;
He, who was so fastidious, so immaculately turned out,
But this, this was the real thing – pain, mutilation, death,
He shivered, feeling the nausea
of fear almost overwhelm him.

5.30 a.m. zero hour, the whistles blew dissipating his fear,
As if rising from the dead, they clambered from the tunnels
Crossing the snow-covered uplands towards their goal.
As in a nightmare, he saw his officer fall,
comrades either side, falter,
But the fear of being left behind, alone, drove him on,
Till it was done and he was safe, untouched and grateful.

Resting behind the lines, he had developed haemorrhoids,
Painful, yet fortuitous – he had been sent to
Blighty to recuperate.
The Concert Party was a mistake, he saw it now.
Evidence of its success was found in a photograph,
Carousing in a white sheet during the 'entertainment'
with the nurses –
Florence was not amused – however
forgiveness was in the air,
On his being passed fit to return to the front,
she was found to be pregnant!

Posted to a different battalion was not easy,
friends had gone, or were dead.

The time at home had tempered the horror,
but not healed it.
He could not talk about it, no-one would understand,
so why try?
Ever sensitive, cultured, an obvious gentleman,
now nearly forty
He found the callow recruits of 1918 a shallow mystery,
But the birth of a daughter in July made
him even more determined to survive-
An unemotional achievement the Forest of
Mormal was privy to,
Not far from where it all began, four long years before.

III

Not until March 1919 did the Army see fit to let him go;
To go back into a world a far cry from the
pre-war haven of peace –
A mere three years, but a lifetime in experience and in pain.
Forty years of age, three, soon to be four children,
and no work
In a land not fit even for losers as it seemed,
let alone heroes-
So he sought occasional comfort and solace
in the time-accustomed manner
Spending what little spare money he had to enter
the world of escape
With kindred souls who wallowed in
self-pity and thought they remembered.

Life seemed to hold no future at this time; he intermittently
talked of lost friends,
Waking sweating in the night babbling more of fear and filth.
After the confessional pub, the pawnbroker
saw more of him than his wife.
Gradually the nightmares faded, or at
least became bearable,

He returned to work as a draper, then
as a clerk in the War Office
And when an ex-Corporal Shicklegruber manifested airs
above his station,
He donned another uniform and
as a resolute and conscientious ARP warden
Nightly patrolled the Blitz-battered south-London streets.

An unlikely soldier he died at the healthy age of eighty-two,
Ever proud of having been a Royal Fusilier, possessor of
Squeak and Wilfred,
Having 'done his bit' for peace, civilisation
and what was right –
What better epitaph can a man have?

*IN PROUD AND LOVING MEMORY OF PTE. E B BRIGGS,
9TH & 11TH ROYAL FUSILIERS – MY GRANDAD.*

Home, Sweet Home

A decorated frieze of brick wall, an open hearth
Evidence once of home, now solitary
sentinels in the shell-swept scene.
Nothing else remained, except a prowling skeletal cat.
Everyone had gone west taking the scanty
remains of their lives
Packed into cart and barrow or atop an aching back.
But in the ancient cellar beneath the stubborn sentinels
Remained the troglodyte remnants of one family.
Each morn emerging, surveying what else the Hun had hit.
They scavenged amongst the detritus of desolation.
Acquiring long-gone neighbours'
clothes to be worn layer on layer;
Foraging for firewood from furniture until
Descending dark drove them into the depths
of the derelict cellar,
Where their solitary light shone beacon-
like amongst the emptiness,
Dreaming of war's end when the invader was beaten.

But it could never be as it was; two sons would never return;
One lost in distant Dardanelles where the heathen
Turk held sway;
The other falling on the rolling scapes of Champagne.
Only Paul remained too young, but not for ever!
There was nowhere to go, so stoically they accepted their lot,
Praying without hope to an irrelevant
God that he would see them through.

As darkness sidled over the invader's trenches on
the nearby hill
Heinrich again adjusted the trajectory of
the evening's final shells;
It had become a matter of professional pride;
That solitary light, amidst the brick sentinels
in the ruins below,
Probably harbouring enemy observers,
machine-guns, who knows,
Whatever, they had to go.
Satisfied at last, he knew as he pulled the trigger
he had finally got it right.

Honourable, but not Artillery

At the funeral service of Lt J H Pritchard and Pte C D Elphick, Honourable Artillery Company, in the presence of HRH Prince Michael of Kent at HAC Cemetery, Ecoust St. Mein, Tuesday 23rd April 2013.

Things work their way to the surface at their own pace,
Determined they will not be forgotten;
Determined to kick-start a memory, a tradition,
a family story.
No-one remembers with certainty,
the participants have faded,
Nothing remains but vestiges of second-hand pain;
A familiar nickname, a faded image
That demands you keep the jumbled heartbeat alive.
Why this is so, is seldom revealed,
Until the strangest of triggers, a French farmer's plough,
Sets in motion the fulfilment, the proof of ages.
A bag of bones means little, but amongst the detritus of death
Shines the key to open the store of remembrance.

A windswept cemetery, white-stone sentinels
Poised to welcome a long lost comrade.
Generations link memories across the years,
Proud, yet hesitant, doing the best they can;
A bizarrely Romanov presence; martial perfection;
Interred with honour, distant tears as the cameras record;
Respectful mourners, in a disrespectful world.
Where across the ages, a plaintive song
Rendered to his mother, from another moment,
A final act of filial love,
Re-echoes across the fields where the
dragon of death once roared.
Now he can rest, as on this day of
St George we pay final homage,
Witnesses that the debt of remembrance is paid.

July 1st 1916

The blackbird's anguished shriek woke him with a start;
Confused by his deep, dream-filled sleep
He struggled to gather his thoughts into cohesion,
Until his gaze fell upon his much chewed pencil
Lying dormant on the muddy duckboard,
Then memories, one tripping over another
In their haste to be remembered
Flooded back and the harsh reality
of the day dawned.

A day born in sunlight and gentle breezes;
A day when they would leave their haven in the earth
And stroll as if in their Sunday
best promenading in the park
Across the emptiness of No Man's Land
To the broken enemy trenches,
Untouchable in parade lines of khaki,
'Half way to Berlin already!'

As phlegmatically he retrieved the errant pencil,
Checking that the folded letter,
'To be opened in the event of my death,'
Was safely in the pocket of the tunic,
A sudden shiver, despite the early summer heat,
Shook his being and he paused.......

Le Bleuet

Bleached by the sun and washed by the rain,
The rib-cage gleamed from the Artois mud;
The shell-shocked sod home to a
tapestry of poppies.
But from the lonely bones a solitary cornflower rose,
A blue beacon, lonely sentinel amongst
the blood-red field.

He had fallen in the first flush of war;
the days of innocence,
Sacrificial canon fodder in those days of naïve valour,
Toy soldiers in red pantaloons and blue tunics,
Overwhelmed by the efficient field grey
of a relentless foe,
Scythed down as they crossed the rolling
fields of Mother France,
In lines abreast braving bullet and shell.

The bullet struck him in his eager, heaving breast,
Falling backwards, unnoticed amongst the slaughter.
Here he lay as Death's relentless process enslaved him.
No martial stone marks his grave, only a lonely name
Carved in the village whence he came;
A name and Nature's eternal remembrance – le bleuet.

Le Jour De Gloire

AUGUST 3RD 1914

Just another summer's day when the world went mad and was
never the same again.
Just another summer's day in every somnambulant French
town and village.
Just another summer's day when many woke with the sun but
would never do so again.
Just another summer's day, except that France was at war!

In every hamlet, village and town throughout the land the
notices suddenly appeared,
WAR DECLARED – MOBILIZATION –
REPORT TO… – VIVE LA FRANCE
It began with an eagerness, an excitement unparalleled, affect-
ing man and boy alike.
So the harvest, a good year, was not gathered in, the War was
much more attractive,
Alsace so long stolen by the Hun, could once more be theirs.

Jules smiled at the memory of the exuberances
of his young friends in the café last night.
He remembered the last time, when the Allemand hordes in
unbridled triumph,
Had rubbed the pretty little nose of Madeleine into the
midden of disgrace,
Taking Alsace for her prize. It was time to repay the debt.

Now with the Motherland threatened
it was necessary to stand and to be counted
To be a loving, loyal enfant of the land that spawned him.
The call had come on Saturday, but Monday
3rd was THE day the madness began,
Gabriella had taken the blue coat, the red
pantaloons from the box in the attic.
Smelling of ancient mothballs, it secretly pleased
him that it still fitted.
Life had been good to him; the boucherie,
a flourishing concern,
But now he must forsake it, his country needed
him and he was ready to go.

It was nearly time for the train to leave,
a momentary lump in the throat
As he kissed the tiny Francoise in her cradle,
rudely dispelled by the other children
Hanging round his neck in a paroxysm
of excitement and sadness.
Gabriella pressed a newly baked pie into his hand,
failing to mask her pain.
Wrapped for the journey, to where he knew not,
but eastwards to the enemy was certain.

Leaving quickly as the emotion threatened to
envelope them all

He joined his neighbours as they marched
towards the station.
In the noon day heat he panted with the rare exertion,
his collar rubbed his neck;
His left boot squeaked in protest;
his pack seemed full of lead –
But exhilaration spurred them on oblivious
to sweat and pain.

In the station the little train wheezed with
importance as they pushed through the cheering crowds,
Clambering aboard, the whistle blew the final trump,
as the last man
Threw his bag into the wooden carriage and was hauled
aboard by willing arms.
Creaking breathlessly, the train gathered
speed as it rounded the first bend.
Jules looked behind him one last time –
the church, the familiar sky-line
Would he ever see them again? Steeling himself he turned his
back on all he loved.

It did not matter; it was his duty, his destiny to fight for
Mother France;
The future held no fears for him, if France died,
he died, leaving nothing but shame and dishonour.

As they approached the first town, the sound greeted them of
a multitude cheering;
The faint strains of the Marseillaise became ever more
distinct, flowing over them
Cajoling them instinctively to join in, until all other sounds
were overwhelmed, the seduction complete –
Allons enfants de la patrie, le jour de gloire est arrive!

Lost at Sea

The strident klaxon call brought the
long-feared dread
As the water-tight doors with fearsome
finality slammed shut;
He felt her presence, imagined her smile,
smelt her very being.
Knowing suddenly he shared
this coffin with her love alone.
It seemed as in a dream he continued his task
His heart pounding to the engine's inexorable beat
Until the awaited impact ceased the diesel's roar
And he was left surrounded by screams.
Stoically sitting on a bench he waited
amidst the panic,
Taking her photo from his pocket
Her familiar face smiled up at him,
Her embrace an imagined reality.
But content she was there, he waited
death's final embrace.

Suddenly she looked up from her tedious day,
A sudden chill encouraging an unwelcome shiver
As the incessant rain beat on the window.
His last letter read through a thousand tears
Open on her desk, the photo hidden in shadow
And with a rising sob, she knew.

Ma Patrie

Abruptly awakened by the cacophonic clatter
of hoof on pavé,
Gerard momentarily glimpsed a cold Teutonic future;
But peering through the frost-begrimed window
He saw the comforting blue of a friendly patrol.
Hastily donning crumpled clothes
he hurried to the central yard.
Dawn was reluctantly, silently creeping over the hill;
the midden stirred;
The garrulous ducks joking their delight at another day.
"Looking for a raiding-party of Uhlans," the Captain smiled,
"They may come this way, mon père. You should leave,
You would not look comfortable on the end
of one of their toys!"
The troop laughed condescendingly, a shallow effort
Knowing there was much bitter truth in the jest.
"Take care, mon vieux." And with sabres gently
rattling, they were gone.

Gerard paused and contemplated his home
"Leave! For countless years since the Spanish had held sway;
When these ancient bricks first saw light of day
His ancestors had tilled this soil, his soil,
Invaders had come, imposed their will
Then like all things had gone and life went on,
unchanged, unchanging.
But now it was different –
An eldest son lying on the battlefield of Lorette;
Jean-Pierre, still a child, last heard of two
months ago at Fort Vaux
And his daughter with child widowed at twenty one!"
He spat defiantly and shrugged his bowed shoulders,
"It is God's will. May he strike the stinking
Boche to oblivion."
Unmoved by the enormity, yet impossibility of this thought
He shuffled back into the familiar haven of the warm kitchen.

On the hill among the solid lines of field-grey
The rising sun glinted on the lances of the restless Uhlans.

Mabel

No-one noticed till the sweet insidious
smell of death
Crept down the green-lino stairs that
led to the attic-flat.
No key could be found amongst the detritus of age
So the hefty fireman called, shouldered his way in,
Frantic to open every paint-stuck window
to clear the miasma.

They found her slumped in her ancient chair
As close to the one-bar fire as comfort allowed,
The television blaring facile lies to an empty audience
A festering poached egg beneath a carpet of blue-bottles.

No-one could remember her name,
they only passed the day
When on the stairs they crossed, she,
tottering to the shops.
All agreed she was a lady, shabbily-dressed,
yet elegant,
Ever polite, a demure smile, a gentle soul, ever alone.

When her weightless shadow had been removed,
the air renewed,
Someone shyly uttered, 'Mabel, that was her name, Mabel,'
All waited for more, but none came, and a sad frustration
filled the void.

A week later at the cemetery chapel overlooking
a mournful sea,
A penetrating drizzle wept as her last refuge
received its final sacrament
In the presence of a bored padre eager for his tea,
The undertaker and a dog-walker sheltering
momentarily to wipe his spectacles.

Clearing the empty flat was easy,
everything straight into the rubbish sack,
Easy perhaps, but a chore as landlord he could do without.
Finally it was done, but for an ancient, much handled tin box-
Something prompted him to open it, hopeful of monetary
reward for his efforts!
Tipping its contents on the bare table it revealed
a hoard of envelopes
Chronologically ordered from September
1914 with 'Field Post Office' stamped,
Each addressed to a Miss Mabel S....;
each privy to a much thumbed letter,
All lovingly tied in neat bunches with blue ribbons.
Opening the topmost missive he sat down to read...

As dusk fell he came to the last letter dated June 1916, there
were no more,
Only some green postcards, and a yellowing newspaper
cutting headed 'Casualties,'
On which the name of 'Lieutenant...the Buffs'
had been carefully circled in pencil.
He sighed, and to himself murmured
'What a silly old bird,'
Sweeping the pile of memories into the
remaining rubbish sack.
As he did, a faded rose petal fluttered
un-noticed to the floor.

On the rolling uplands of the Somme, not eighty miles away
In a lonely, windswept cemetery as the
watery sun crept over the horizon,
The last petal on an English rose fell slowly to the ground
Settling gently before the well-worn
headstone simply inscribed
'An Unknown Lieutenant of the East Kent Regiment.'

MCMXVI *Gallipoli*

Chill of a new dawn, a new day, a new year
The mist shrouds the nullah that leads to Krithia
Krithia – the battalion killing fields
So few left from that far-off April dream
A dream so full of promise, Krithia, Constantinople...
A stroll across the fields, Johnny Turk's no fighter!
The Vineyard shattered that lie
All that is left among the blasted vines
Are the rotting vintage of an iron harvest.

The Scotties who were in these trenches before
Yesterday, last year, does it matter?
In thick Glaswegian tones
Told us that it was quiet,
Just keep your head down
Johnny may not celebrate Hogmanay
And does not take a wee dram!
But he's a fair fighter.
"Good luck lads," and they were gone.

Tomorrow or the day after it will be our turn
To trek stealthily down to 'W' Beach
Like guilty trespassers,
Now is not the time to die – when is!
But leaving without so many is so hard-
Walter at Suvla – a good lad, a stout friend
It breaks my heart, but....

A desultory shell loops its way towards Helles.

Mud

The shell landed not five yards from him
The cloying mud deadened its power
But the nearness of death un-nerved him,
He stumbled, slipping on the greasy duckboard
Plunging into the slime-filled shell hole,
His pack dragging him helpless into the depths.
In the inky darkness, the driving rain,
The maelstrom of madness
No-one saw him fall, nor heard his dying screams
As the unforgiving mud held him close till
Eager death enfolded him.

He had been no stranger to mud,
Born in the salubrious slums of Rotherhithe
Spitting distance from the fecund Thames
Where the sliver of tide-created shore
Was his playground, his treasure trove;
Larking about in this porridge of adventure,
The delights of discovery never failed him

As everything lost strove its way to the surface;
Many a dead dog, a begrimed rat
Even, once, a naked, blubbery corpse!

Passchendaele 1917, here the mud was the world;
His totality, encompassing all,
Sticky, glutinous, cloying, it embraced its victims.
Spewing the bitter harvest of corpses.
To fall into a shell-hole was the end of hope;
A false step on a slippery duckboard
Was to drown, to die, to disappear,
Sucked into the miasmic mud......
But not for our Cockney mudlark, he boasted,
'Born in mud, raised on mud', it held no fears for him.
'Let the gas shells fall, let it rain cats and dogs,
Nuffin bothers us London lads,
Not like them bleedin' Northerners,
I'll be all right Jack, no problem.'

Bullshit!

No Laughing Matter

The Anafarta Spur – they'd laughed,
when they heard its name,
Schoolboy humour, immature sniggering –
men never grow up!
But a more serious matter in the way – Scimitar Hill.
Johnny Turk called it Yusufcuk Tepe, Dragonfly Hill,
But it seemed an inappropriate name,
there was nothing delicate,
As it spewed a constant rain of death,
a brooding presence,
Scimitar-shaped, its martial name wholly apt.

They waited in the furnace of a summer's night,
James drank from his bottle, warm,
a hint of petrol, but all there was.
His life in Salford where the sun
was an infrequent visitor
Seemed like another world; only
a two week voyage away

But a lifetime in experience. They landed at Helles.
Then the move to Suvla Bay, a period of calm,
before the storm,
Seaside and shells, but not the piscatorial kind!

On the twentieth day, the move, the battle loomed,
He gulped another mouthful;
he was eager, but a twinge of fear,
Made him glance at his comrades, tough,
resolute Border men,
His fear allayed, he fixed his bayonet and waited...

5.15 and the order came, into the deep,
rocky gullies they poured,
Gullies where the heat collected, the progress
painful, tortuous,
Enfilade fire decimating them, leaving few untouched.
James still lies in those rock-strewn graves,
far from Salford's mills;
His body at one with the barren soil, gone, but not forgotten,
As the dragonflies still gently play on the warm breeze,
Above Suvla Bay near the Anafarta Spur.

In memory of Pte. James Henry Lockley 6th. Border Regt killed in action Scimitar Hill, 9th August 1915, remembered on the Helles Memorial, Gallipoli.

Ode to Walter

In memory of Pte. Walter King 1st Essex Regt of Berden, Essex, killed in action 25th October 1915, buried Azmak Cemetery, Suvla, Gallipoli.

Verdant lanes lead out of the village,
A farmer's cart dawdles to the station,
At once the old rurality fades and London beckons
Arriving open-mouthed into a turmoil of noise
That threatens the desire to sleep, but loses.
Another tired train, back to back houses
Squalid gardens of sorry weeds fade into
Green reminders of home sliding comfortingly by
Till the edge is reached, the mighty ocean.
Cramped into foul reeking holds
Vomit and sleep tossed together until one day the sun
Reflecting in the mill-pond lapping on distant shores
Peaceful days, but ever alert for death beneath the waves
Then secure at last in Mudros Bay
Now the pulse quickens, another Trojan skirmish awaits

Says our officer reciting someone called Homer
As transfer to beetle craft gingerly beckons
Christ it's hot! A curving beach, the crack of shrapnel
Here we go over the side, nearly going under
The pack's like lead, gaining feet, gasping breath
Here, shit-scared, sweating fear.
Dusty trenches beckon, constant hail of bullets
Johnny Turk's irritable today
Cosy thoughts of The Raven, another pint, Bertha...
Blackness, a shallow hole, Azmak.

Oh Lucky Man!

The enemy trenches spewed gun-fire as they advanced;
Men fell beside him but it seemed his life was charmed
As determinedly he pressed on, Twelve Tree Copse ahead.
But it was too good to last, the inevitable
bullet creased his brow;
He stumbled and fell, the blood trickling into his eyes,
Mingling with the sweat of effort and of fear.
He lay still slowly realising he was not dead;
Nausea suddenly rose in his gorge and he vomited;
His already dry throat desperate for the easing balm of water.

All was still now the battle had moved on and raged ahead,
A solitary nightingale gave vent to song above him;
As he looked about him – gnarled olive trees,
dry earth on which lay
The mis-shapen figures captured in death, once his comrades
Now mere shells of humanity, dust to dust.
The sounds of Turkish counter-attack
concentrated his feverish mind

As he crawled into the sanctuary of a nearby dugout
Where he lay as the 'stiff and confused fighting'
passed him by.
When night fell the realisation that he was lost
behind enemy lines
Dawned painfully and he slept and pondered.

At home his parents' grief at the news
he was 'posted missing,'
Was assuaged by the arrival of his last, hastily-penned missive
Informing them he was still, 'A1,' and for them
to 'Keep heart,'
So they waited, fearful, yet hopeful, Alfred's luck
would see him through
And it did, with the help of his hard rations!
One long month he lay un-noticed in this lonely dug-out
Until the ground was re-taken and he emerged unkempt,
Near-delirious, but alive, ready to fight another day.

Lady Luck continued her passionate affair with Alfred,
1916 saw him on the Somme where in the early
stages of the battle
Another wound failed to interrupt his good fortune;
Even a slight graze in March 1917 did not hinder him,
But then the fickle finger of Fate decided he had
pushed it too far.
Uncut German wire, ground raked by machine-gun fire,
Meant another 'missing' letter, this time with a tragic finality.
Alfred's luck had run out and the killing fields of
Picardy are his grave.

*A TRUE STORY – IN MEMORY OF Corporal Alfred William
COX, 9th. Essex Regiment, killed in action April 9th. 1917.
Commemorated on the Arras Memorial to the Missing*

Old Soldiers Fade Away

The lead soldiers were his world
Red tunics, freshly painted, policed his imagination
In the sepulchral nursery where he played alone.
Father, a busy practice to maintain
Called in to chat awkwardly every evening
As the elderly maid served his tea in silence.
Mother, a shadowy wraith, had died before
memory blossomed
Now sustained only by the sepia photographs in the lounge.

So it was inevitable that his solitude continued;
School where his loneliness was only compounded
When the occasional stilted letter came.
Bullied, he sought refuge in the books he read,
Rider Haggard, Buchan and the gloomy Pole, Conrad,
Until release opened endless vistas for adventure.
The vast prairies of Canada and
a lonely farm supplied his needs.
But this was not to be, war for the first time touched him;
South Africa beckoned and a Mounted Rifleman he became
Until a Boer bullet curtailed that dream.

Undeterred by wounding, across the oceans, driven,
The land of the long white cloud beckoned
But the world had developed the taste for war,
Kaiser Bill duly obliged and he was prepared,
Enlisting eagerly and enjoying the delights of
Gallipoli, another irritating wound here,

Egypt and France until Death held him in her clutches.
He yielded not, triumphing over her power,
But at a cost... . .the doctor decreed one eye was not enough
No longer could he a soldier be.

Released from pain and duty he again sought renewal
Half-blind he may be, but a soldier he would always be.
To Canada he returned and a sympathetic doctor
Signed his death sentence with a condescending smile.
France seduced him to her bosom
But Death would not give him a second chance –
He fell, as the advance to victory gathered momentum,
Not three months from the Armistice.
They found him, it seemed with a slight smile on his face
As if his journey was done and he rested content
'He'd gone to his Gawd like a soldier.'

Based on the life of Arthur Norman Hackney, Private, who was killed in action 9th August 1918, age 36 with the 29th Bn, Canadian Infantry (British Columbia Regiment) Born in England, the son of Alfred Hackney MRCS. Served in the South African Campaign then enlisted in 1914 in NZEF, serving in Gallipoli (wounded), Egypt and France where he was blinded in one eye and discharged unfit. Returned to Canada where he re-enlisted in the Mounted Rifles served in France where near Rosieres, he was killed in July 1918.

GRANTED LEAVE–PROMOTED
HAVING DONE HIS BIT

On Leave

The old house creaked comfortingly;
And in this haven from birth the fire spat;
His reverie disturbed, he stirred
Unsure for a brief eternity where he was.
The vivid reality of the smoke-filled trench
receded in his memory
Once more he was in the familiar parlour of home,
A sudden chill enveloped him, cordite was in his nose
Harshly reminding him of his other existence,
A duty beckoning him inexorably on the morrow
Across the narrow sea to the desolation of doom.
Upstairs she slept her breathing untroubled,
Unaware of this other life he could not forget,
Could not begin to talk of; to even grasp –
A life that drew him mercilessly to its fatal bosom.
He leant forward and gently stirred the fading embers
The old house creaked again,
Reluctant to let him go

Ordered to Die

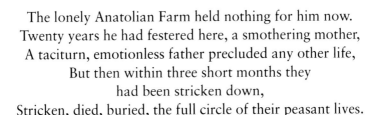

The lonely Anatolian Farm held nothing for him now.
Twenty years he had festered here, a smothering mother,
A taciturn, emotionless father precluded any other life,
But then within three short months they
had been stricken down,
Stricken, died, buried, the full circle of their peasant lives.

The Imam decided his future, there was no question,
The Infidel had come; his homeland needed his service.
So he had gone, to what he knew not, but it had seemed right.
The small farm, lost amidst the vast, anonymous plains,
Forgotten as soon as the corner was turned.

It seemed the Ingilizce threatened far away,
So began the great adventure, training, transportation,
Seemingly endless train days across the
vastness they were protecting
To Constantinople, known only from picture books,
Now a reality, a teeming, dream-like reality.

Then another train, another tedious journey until night fell;
At last the ground beneath their feet; the order to march,
To march and halt the invader, before it was too
late and all would be lost.
Kemal, their officer, a hard, resolute man,
respected, but feared.
'I am not ordering you to attack, I am ordering you to die.'

Thus the day of martyrdom arrived, a day to fight and die.
To stop the khaki hordes from stealing his homeland.
Strangely they had not pushed forward
through the empty gap,
Surely Allah smiled on him as the enemy
swam and laughed on the beach
As busy boats plied to and fro,
bringing the ingredients of war.

Watching from the hastily-dug trench, the unforgiving August
sun at its peak,
He wondered if Allah had decided on his martyrdom;
The farm, the only life he had known had gone,
this was all he had left.
Looking down the trench at his comrades
and the cold-eyed officer, Kemal
It hinted at a new order of things, a new direction.

But first it was necessary to survive;
it was not the time for his martyrdom.
The strident call to 'Fix Bayonets,' shattered his absorption
As he rose from the trench the cry of
'Allah' poured from a thousand throats.

Peace on Earth 1914

He gazed across the arid space of no man's land
Covered by a dilatory mask of snow
Empty yet threatening in the harsh light of a winter sun.
A hostile pitch away he felt the unseen eyes, vigilant;
Eyes that earlier in another lifetime it seemed,
Had looked in his with warmth and amity.

The day of Christ's birth had dawned weakly;
The guns were stilled as if by seasonal thoughts of home.
Fuelled by the insidious smell of bacon cooking
Which crept into the psyche of these men desirous of peace.
This dreamlike reverie suddenly rent by familiar words
'Happy Christmas, Tommy!'
Familiar yet surprising from whence it came;
Not unwelcome, but in its unexpectedness shocking.

Then a distant figure climbed confidently from the devils' lair
Holding aloft a tepid flag of truce.
'Don't trust the bastard Boche,' was stilled by curious voices

And a procession of inquisitive pilgrims
Clambered hesitantly from the haven of their trenches
To meet, Brandenberger and Tommy in tentative goodwill.

Now all was over, his Teutonic friend,
One-time waiter in the Strand, father of two
(with humble pride he had showed their photo)
Had returned promising never to fight again.
Incredulous in the morning's unfriendly chill,
He wondered if the dream of yesterday could be true-
A new day, peace on earth?
He sought the comfort of her photo cocooned in
the pocket near his heart.

Sudden darkness enveloped him as the daily hate
Blew to pieces the errant dream.
The kindly letter returned with the blood-stained photo
Told the her the perpetual lie –
'He died immediately, he suffered no pain,,,,;

Perfidious Albion

It was his fault, he should have gone when he could.
Instead he dawdled, the army assembled,
but the chance had gone.
Only an Imperial Eagle's throw away and it would have been
the Emperor's crowning prize.
But Perfidious Albion lived up to her name.
All that remained was the Column to his dreams.
There he stood, le P'tit Caporal, looking away in shame
Away from his unobtainable goal,
White-cliffed, resolute, unsullied.
No wonder 'Punch' mocked him, 'His back still turned
Upon that land that never saw his face.'.

This had not been the first time, that
damned march to Moscow.
Again he was at fault; the weather he had no control over,
But again he hesitated and all was lost.
He blamed his many ailments, but in truth,
The supplies ran out, the cold gnawed at their very souls

And he abandoned them and they knew it!
No column forthcoming for that!

Yet how fickle fate played her hand and all that was, was not;
The ancient foe became the friend.
Perfidious no longer the khaki hordes crossed La Manche,
Marching, singing and happy to die for France,
Which they dutifully did in disciplined lines!
No resentment, for them the past was another country,
Hearing their strange tongues as they marched past
Shouting out grotesque but amicable greetings,
'Come to 'elp you, Boney, you don't deserve it,
you old Corsican
But we can't let that bloody 'un get his way.'
And they were gone.

Atop his column he waited, as they returned
Aware behind him as they populated the newly dug cemetery
Between his lofty pinnacle, the sea and their home.
White headstones, identical rows, no privileges,
no burial by rank
Just beardless poilus from across the
piece of water he would never cross.
The little man from Corsica atop his column smiled
He had achieved his wish, they were his enfants
Let them rest eternally in his care – Vive les Anglais!

The Column of the Grande Armée is a 53 metre high triumphal column (modelled on Trajan's Column in Rome) with Napoleon atop overlooking Terlincthun British Cemetery. The column was intended to commemorate a successful invasion of England (an invasion that never occurred).

Plane Trees

As he crested the brow of the next identical hill
Seeing the interminable road rise and
fall into the August haze,
For the first time he noticed the avenue of plane trees
Regimentally planted at regular intervals along the road
Providing occasional welcome shade in the stifling heat.
Familiar to him, he suddenly recalled the suburban road
Where he was born and lived, another time, another world,
But a world where outside the house on the pavement
Stood a large plane tree, shading the house and garden,
But also the source of a multitude of boyish pleasures –
Picking off the peeling bark, as good as
the scabs on his knees;
Carving his initials in the exposed yellowish skin,
Later adding a heart and those of the buxom girl from
number two,
Whom he shyly admired from afar, occasionally
rewarded by her smile.
His reverie was broken by the stentorian tones of the CSM,
'Right you lot, ten minutes rest, one mouthful of water.
Still a long way to go and those bloody
Huns ain't far behind.'
Sitting down in the shade he became aware of the hardships
of the retreat –
His tunic had rubbed his sunburnt neck raw;
His unfeeling boots the cause of throbbing blisters
Three days' worth since they
had forsaken the slagheaps of Mons.

Many a good mate had been left there dead, wounded or lost;
Many had fallen by the wayside, march or die was the order.
But he knew without doubt that he would make it safely
Despite the heat, the pavé and the pursuing Uhlan cavalry
Ready and eager to stick him without compunction.
He became aware as these thoughts traversed his weary mind
That he was peeling the bark from a so-familiar plane tree,
Without a second thought he drew his bayonet
from his scabbard
Carefully carving 'T A'and '26 August 1914'
on the exposed tree.
Satisfied, the order to move, before the
ever-following Hun appeared,
Troubled him little; he was up ready for the
ten kilometres to Landrecies.
He paused, pulling a piece of speckled
bark from the ancient tree
Placing it gently in his tunic pocket,
He smiled, turned and strode ever south.

Rain

The spider crawled purposely towards his open collar;
He could see it, but was powerless to stop it,
As it disappeared, he could feel its tentacles,
Knowing it would soon bite, and that would be that.
He woke with a start bathed in a chilly sweat
As the persistent rain trickled down his neck.

Pulling himself together, he inwardly laughed,
Mocking his childhood phobia of everything insect
Seeming of little importance now beside a 5.9er!
He surveyed his domain; it was easy to describe –
Mud, mud and more mud.
glutinous, ubiquitous, turgid;
His feet perpetually in fetid water,
A Bosch coal-scuttle helmet, still brain-bespattered
Peeping through a malodorous puddle,
A large hole in it, gaping at him, mocking him,
Persuading him to dwell on his flimsy mortality.

The habitual evening 'Hate' was late tonight,
A few more hours of the creeping, insidious drizzle;
He shivered as the rain grew harder.
Late it might be, but more baleful was the prospect,
As if the Hun blamed him personally for the rain!
But until then he could drowse
Ignoring the incessant dripping down his neck
From his helmet – protection from the errant shard
But useless at keeping him dry.

He closed his eyes, dreaming of her warm, buxom body,
All thoughts of disagreeable arachnids quelled in his reverie,
Blissfully unaware of the spider above him
Descending on a gossamer cord towards
his unbuttoned tunic,
And his 'designated' shell being slid into its barrel
At that very moment – and still it rained.

Retreat from Mons

As they crested yet another hill, seeing with despair
The now so familiar tableau, the straight,
never-ending route
Climbing to rise after rise as far as their
weary eyes could see
It became apparent that the relentless,
pursuing Uhlans
Were the least of their enemies.
Three new insidious threats occupied their minds –
Tiredness, the August heat and the unforgiving pavé.

Six hours they had marched from Mons,
ever southwards,
Their shirts beneath the heavy khaki,
sticking to their backs;
Their boots, hobnail-torture,
hiding blood-soaked socks;
Hands still clenched around their rifles
which had served them well –

Fifteen rounds a minute had culled the grey
Hun hordes,
But it was not enough and retreat was ordered,
Six long hours ago.

At first a sense of disciplined panic
drove them on, and on,
But as the eternal straight road and safety
hypnotised their efforts
They became aware only of the
pain ruling their thoughts.
Wren, one-time legionnaire in another life,
to escape a "crime passsionel",
Muttered as he marched, marched and muttered,
'March or die.'
'March or die,' till he was abruptly told to 'shut it.'

There were only four of the platoon left now;
The comfort of the wayside shade had lured some,
'We'll catch up, don't worry,'
echoed meaningless in their ears.
Finding the bottles of cognac in the empty house
Was too much for Diggory, ever eager for a drink….
But the four kept going, the khaki musketeers,
Brothers-in-arms since the days on the high veldt.

Mormal loomed ahead, perhaps a refuge
deep in its forest depths,
But even on a summer's day,
a sense of foreboding permeated
Too easy to lose the way, be ambushed by field-grey
But also a decision to be made which road to take,
where was sanctuary?
Resolute in their task,
once made the decision Le Cateau
Eased their need to think, just to march –

So they marched, till they stumbled,
stumbled till they fell and
The sleep of exhaustion overwhelmed them.

Waking, under a sun fiery already,
they marched and stumbled
Ever wary of the pursuant Hun,
but convinced of their invincibility,
Marched and stumbled, four Contemptible
Comrades together
As the heat haze shimmered over the ruler-straight road,
Disappearing into an unknown future where
their destiny beckoned
Accepted, uncomplaining, inevitable,
To fight another day.

Retribution

I

Moonlight, a balmy night stirred an unlikely playfulness,
As he cycled home, taking the normally
muddy track by Snails Farm.
Tonight the bumpy incline beckoned, stretching out his
be-clipped legs,
He free-wheeled uttering long dormant voices of childhood,
When suddenly the summer stillness was
shattered by the whir of engines,
The stutter of gunfire as a huge shadow passed over him,
Becoming a sphere of fire as it crashed
uncontrolled into the fields beyond.

II

Oberleutnant Peterson cursed the searchlights
as they illuminated the sky;
Anti-aircraft barrages burst dangerously close to
his vulnerable craft;

There was no choice as he turned the monster
towards Fatherland and safety.
He had no innate feeling of morality as he
off-loaded his bombs
Five tons of death from the firmament
dumped on civilian Purfleet
As the last fell, his satisfaction was momentary
as from nowhere a stream of bullets
Tore open the side and in a cylindrical ball
of flame it fell to earth.

III

1 a.m. the patrol was over, another quiet routine night,
the sky his playground,
Scouting for marauders, fruitless it seemed yet again,
he sighed,
A sigh abruptly curtailed by a Zeppelin,
caught in the corner of his eye,
Below him heading eastwards, unaware,
confident in its power, its size.
He noticed the last bombs falling indiscriminately below,
Angry but with an icy coolness,
he dived and with his guns blazing vengeance
Watched with horrified satisfaction as the
leviathan exploded and fell.

IV

Dropping his bike, it seemed as if the solitary
assassin exhibited a victory roll for him
As it disappeared in triumph, he remembered
his duty and he ran towards the inferno.
News spread as quickly as the fire and
out of the gloom came a gathering audience
Hushed with delight; eager to see the mighty fallen;
eager to claim a souvenir

Leaving their bicycles strewn across the
fields as if in homage and supplication.
The behemoth was mastered,
a Goliath struck down by the solitary David
Retribution exacted, the bringer of
Death from the skies tamed.

Reverie on 'Bert

Insidiously the rain seeped down their necks
As they crested the rise and halted above the shattered town.
Never pretty in peace it now resembled
a Dante-esque descent into Hell;
Peephole views into ravaged, desolate homes
An unmade bed, a legless chair,
a broken photograph upon a wall.
A dishevelled cur barked feebly
and slunk away into the maze of night.
Insidiously the rain seeped down their necks.

Their reverie was interrupted by a voice exclaiming,
'Ain't that the church, there, you know the one,
Where when that statue, the one on its side falls
This bleedin' war will end – you know the Virgin.'
'That'll be the first one I've seen in this bloody country!'
Sniggered someone at the rear,
and a ripple of mirth flowed as
Insidiously the rain seeped down their necks.

Then silence returned, all enveloped in thoughts
Praying for a purposeful projectile
To demonstrate the legend to be true,
Whilst towards their destination
Thiepval to the north-west
The waiting firmament flashed and
the greedy expectant guns grumbled as
Insidiously the rain seeped down their necks.

Secret Love

For the first time he felt a pang of sadness, of regret
As he gazed over the rolling hills to Kaipara
Harbour and the sea.
This farm had been his solitary obsession for seven years,
Here he had toiled till he dropped,
falling asleep in his chair at dinner,
Creating a home, but no-one to share it with.
But he did not mind, he loved solitude,
preferring his own company.
As a pupil at the Boys' British School, he had had few friends,
An elder brother who shunned
the opportunity to come with him.
Then the war came, but so far away it mattered little
Until soon the papers wrote of Gallipoli and Chunuk Bair
Publishing lists of the dead, sons, brothers,
fathers he casually knew.
Letters from home replicated this sorrow, in France,
Wipers, the Dardanelles
Walter at Suvla, Lewis from up the road,
schoolmates. . . . .many others –
He knew he must go, leave his lonely
life's work, his farm,
Despite his age, to cross the unbounded ocean to 'do his bit,'

On leave in his brother's house, his life was reborn;
Her golden hair, her scent, the warmth of her breath
As she leaned over him to serve his dinner
Captivated him, entranced him and he knew for the first time.

Desolation – she was his brother's wife!
The only solace was that, to his delight,
their love was mutual,
Impossible to stop, but necessary to conceal.
A stolen kiss, a solitary golden hair upon his sleeve
Treasured, placed carefully in his military-issue bible,
Forever testament to their eternal love.
Precious days passed all too quickly; the Bull Ring beckoned,
Whispered words of love, a hurried kiss was all they shared.
A carriage took him to the station; through the rear window
Her golden hair shimmered, then faded as
she receded into the distance.

The searing hot blast of the shell hurled him to the ground
Shrapnel searing, piercing his breast and he screamed
A primal scream silenced only by the darkness
that enveloped him.
A gentle murmur, punctuated by strident cries
of pain awoke him
By his bed a white-robed doctor pointing,
sadly shaking his head.
In that nether time between waking and sleeping, he was
moved to a quiet corner.
It mattered not, she would come for him.
Dusk fell and suddenly out of the gloom, she was there,
Running, her golden hair streaming behind her,
catching the fading light;
Behind her, his brother, smiling, waving to him from afar
He stretched out his arms to clasp her, never to let her go
Tears of joy as she came closer, ever closer.................
The orderly checked for his silent pulse,
closed his staring eyes
Wiping a solitary tear from his contented cheek,
Pulling the coarse blanket over his lifeless face.

In Loving Memory of Rifleman C 'Tom' SMITH (75208) 1st. New Zealand Rifle Brigade, died of wounds October 8th. 1918, aged 39 after just eight days in the front-line . Buried Delsaux Farm Cemetery, Beugny,

Silence in the Sky

The insidious cold woke him, he shivered uncontrollably,
Pulling his great coat up to his chin, dawn not yet awake,
He dozed and dreamed, dreamed and dozed
Places and faces crowded into view, all gone now,
Dead or wounded, all but fifty who landed at Gallipoli
Three and a half years and a lifetime ago.
Yet in just over six hours rumour had it would be over,
At the eleventh hour of the eleventh month,
Some twenty-five miles to the south-west of Mons,
Where the first shots of the war were fired,
Little dreaming that there would be four Christmases before
The nightmare ended, a future as yet unknown;
A future where nothing would be as before.

They had talked of this day in many a candle-lit dugout
Shell-strafed and doubting it would ever be,
But now it was almost here. When the last gun fired
Nothing would change, it was out of place to celebrate
After so much sacrifice, so many friends lost –

Walter, at Suvla, too eager to demonstrate
Bertha's ample charms,
Sniped through his day-dreams; Sid, ever eager Sid,
First over the top, first to fall at Beaumont-Hamel.
William, the stoic, steadfastly avoiding shell and bullet
But falling prey to trench fever,
sent home and never returning.
Tom on a stifling summer day cut in half by
rattling machine gun fire
Falling, flailing arms, a look of shock upon his open face
Then lying motionless in the August heat
Disappearing forever in the shell blasted fields of Artois.

So it is each Armistice Day, when the stored memories
Of heroism, selflessness, of effort and above all comradeship
Even to the extent of sacrificing life for the sake of friends,
Are dusted off, not shared but
remembered with sadness and pride,
The un-aging faces that shall not grow old –
Walter, Sid, William, Tom

The Adrian Helmet

Louis Adrian's new helmet shone in the September sun
As every poilu donned its 700 grams of steel
Throwing away with abandon the cap of comfortable cloth.

Auguste pulled his hard down on his head
As the evening bombardment peppered the front-line trench
White hot shrapnel bouncing like peas on a drum
No match for the Adrian helmet.

Shiny bright blue it had arrived; too bright for comfort
Until it had been lovingly passed through the mud
Until gaudy no longer, stained, yet familiar.

Adjusting the leather strap till it bit into his neck
Auguste hypnotically responded to the whistle
Clambering reluctantly from the trench
Into the blast that tore his helmet from his shattered head
Adding another stain to the battered casque.

Behind him, inexplicably helmetless,
Henri clutched desperately at the still warm Adrian
Frantically seeking sanctuary beneath its sticky steel,
But too late the staccato bullets exploded into his head
Covering the vestiges of blue in the gruesome gore of death.

In Artois the poilus' discarded Adrian
lies broken in the mud
In Paris Louis Adrian proudly polishes
his new Legion d'honneur!

The Birthday Cake

She buried it in the garden, tearful but resolute,
Determined her anguish would ease once it had gone.
It had been returned in the same box, soiled but intact,
The day before, releasing a flood of raw pain
and withheld memories.
She had secreted it to her room without a word to anyone.
Where in this sanctuary her uncontrolled tears fell freely
In a baptism of grief.

It had been a creation of love, to remember his birthday;
His first away from her carefully nurtured nest;
He who had been born through such pain;
He who had survived against the odds, her only child.
Carefully wrapped to withstand the travails of the journey
His favourite, to ease the pain of parting,
to keep her love remembered.
The sudden telegram shattered everything;
her world fell apart;
Her darling little boy was no more

Weeks passed and she hid her pain deep in her soul;
Only the silent looking-glass in her room witness to her tears,
Elsewhere she wore the mask of acceptance
Until it was returned, unopened, not shared by his comrades
And her fortitude crumbled; her pain knew no bounds.
Until one dark night she resolved her dilemma.
She took the still unopened package and with
her memories, her pain,

She buried them deep in the garden, watered by her tears.
Never to be mentioned again.

*In Memory of Pte Aubrey W Hayward 11th Essex 12.10.1918
buried Busigny Communal Cemetery Extension. A true story.*

The Cavalry Charge

Medieval knights in Adrian helmets;
Lances poised eagerly aloft ready for Boche-sticking;
Poilus in beardless conformity seeking manhood
Callow-faced, yet ready to die, they know not why,
Only to follow the hysterical white charger
Biting its bit in a frenzy of hyper-activity.
Their disinterested nags look wistfully
For solace in the verdant pasture underfoot.
They know the game – graze when you can.
Suddenly the trump of doom destroys this reverie
Gathered up in a paroxysm of energy, they charge;
The downhill pace quickens
Till the world has stopped and nothing remains
But the sound of speed
On, on the legs outpace the mount
Leaving nothing but staccato sounds of
the reaper's deadly welcome
That rip and tear till the poilu-enfants astride their carousel
Lie heaped in bloody abortive sacrifice
As one with the naked soil of Mother France.

The Commandant

The dilatory Spring sun slid slowly in the west;
The awakening garden still visible before her
Once a haven from the horror of the trenches
Where minds and limbs were mended
But now it was over, the last man had gone
As they had all done before – over one thousand souls
Repaired, renewed, ready for a return to the fray
Or the Blighty escape of 'unfit for service.'
All that is but one –it irritated her sense of perfection.
A sigh escaped as she opened the photo album on her desk –
There she was, mirror image smiling back,
The Commandant resplendent on the first day,
Nearly four years and a life-time ago.
'Commandant' – it had always sat uneasily with her
Discordant, so martial, so cold when she
was so tender, so warm.
She slowly turned the pages,
relishing each memory they stirred –
The fine old house in 1915
poised ready to treat the first convoy,
A group of eager nurses, expectant,
confident in their healing power.
How she remembered that first day, waiting at the station
As the ponderous train from
Dover laden with its fragile cargo,
Amidst the smell of steam and the
noise of vociferous porters
Crept to a halt, disgorged its load
into the waiting ambulances;

The short, slow drive down the High Street,
past inquisitive onlookers;
Arrival and the form C2, a roll call of abbreviated
diseases and injuries –
G.S.W, S.W, I.C.T and later the all-encompassing P.U.O
As well as gassed, fractures and the mysterious albuminuria,
A sombre litany of war's obscene power.
A small frown crossed her pretty, open face
Remembrance of another unwelcome
entry in the last column – V.D.H
Her boundless sympathy ceased here, self-inflicted
They should be elsewhere not with her heroes, men of honour,
She inwardly laughed at her sudden pomposity,
it was her duty!
Another page revealed another convoy,
Photos recalled; names and faces from across the Empire;
Nurses, who naïve at first, gained skills, moved on
To military hospitals where death held sway, but angels trod.
But some who stayed holding the first hands in 1915;
Waving a tearful farewell as the last one left.
As she turned the pages, the years passed by,
until the dusk impeded
Reluctantly she closed the album,
keeping her memories safe;
Drawing the curtains, she took one last
look at the disappearing garden
And shut the door on her life, her past.
Momentarily standing outside she glanced at the sign
For the first time in four years its incongruity had at last gone
She was, had been, and always would be
The Commandant.

P.U.O.- *One of the final medical challenges of the Great War
was the influenza pandemic which started in the Spring of
1918. There was some confusion as to whether this disease was
influenza and prior to this fact being established troops who*

succumbed were marked, P.U.O – Pyrexia of Unknown Origin – persistent or recurring fever.

Albuminuria is a pathological condition wherein albumin is present in the urine. It is a type of proteinuria

V.D.H. – A polite way of suggesting he was to be transferred to a Venereal Disease Hospital

I.C.T. – Inflammation Connecting Tissue. I.C.T. was a general term for suppurating skin diseases (Pyodermia)

G.S.W – Gun Shot Wound

S.W – Shell Wound

The Ghost Cart

The road shone steel-grey in the crisp winter moonlight
As Joe walked the familiar, yet interminable
way from Pop to Ypres.
The stark, skeletal trees; the occasional wayside cemetery, the
Only real manifestations he noticed on his Via Dolorosa,
That and in the distance, Wipers,
glowing in the black night sky,
The rhythmic thudding of shell-fire the only sound of war;
Suddenly his reverie was broken by
the reverberation of trotting
Converging in the inky night, till suddenly it was there –
A mule drawn mess-cart lumbering straight at him.
Standing aside to let it past, a sudden shiver shook his frame –
The obedient, jogging beast was driverless!
Instinctively he snatched the flailing bridle
Bringing the mule to a sudden, unscheduled halt.
Standing patiently, its sides gently heaving, it waited
As he looked inside the open cart,
where filling the whole back,
A large blanket, covered by a huge stain of crimson gore
On which lay a severed head,
the battered helmet still in place!
Joe cried out, stepping back in horror and as he did
The four-footed, equine soldier tossed his head,
as if to say 'enough,'
Tore the bridle from his grasp and bolted into the dark.
Left to the empty road and his thoughts,
Joe continued on his way,

Until the sombre lights of Vlamertinghe came into view.
Approaching the village, from the darkness of the Hop Store,
A disembodied voice challenged
him and he blurted out his tale.
The voice grimly laughed, 'Oh, that's old Mike.
He appears often.'
Continuing cheerfully, 'They say,
if you meet him, your number's up!
I haven't seen him, but many have, so take care.'
With that he was gone, leaving Joe to his troubled thoughts.
The desolate highway shone steel-grey
in the crisp winter moonlight.

In Memory of Private Joseph Albert BRAYBROOKE (PW 187) 18th. Middlesex Regiment, (Pioneers. The 1st. Public Works Battalion), died of wounds 1st. March 1916, aged 36.

In February, 1916, Albert came home on leave for seven days. On leaving he said goodbye to his mother remarking that he felt he would never see her again. Tragically, his premonition was true. On his way back to the trenches, behind the lines, he was killed by a stray shell..

The Hero

They found him by the withered tree
Bones enmeshed in its gnarled roots
White, picked clean and some whole,
The vacant skull, teeth grinning,
A neat round hole above the accusing sockets.
'Sniped. Left where he fell, poor bugger,'
The man from Beaurains said with relish.
He dug cursorily, filled a bucket with bones
Fragments enough to fill three more in fact,
Then laying them out into a matchstick man.
He opined wisely, 'Enough for a burial,
Deserves that doesn't he?
They were all heroes, weren't they.'

Had they seen him, hiding, running
From the shells, the bullets, even his mates;
Seen him scratching, spitting, screaming, kicking
As they held him, an obscene feral beast
Personified by filthy oaths,

The stench of fear-soiled clothes
Until in desperation the callow youth who was their officer
Took it from his holster, held it to his crazed head
Eyes closed, pulled the reluctant trigger.
Into a water-logged hole our hero slid
Under the withered tree,
'Good riddance, bastard. This is what you deserve.'

The Knock at the Door

The persistent knocking at the door awoke her,
Weakly, she struggled to rise, calling out his name,
Crying at her inability to answer the insistent sound,
Convinced after all these years he had come at last.
Gently the nurse laid her down, wiping her burning brow,
'He'll come soon,' she lied, hoping to ease her agitation,
To settle her into sleep; the sleep of release.
Four simple words that concealed a lifetime of heartbreak.

Two years he had been gone from her, a proud Pompadour,
When dead men's shoes needed filling to plug the gaps,
In their martial wisdom, posted from the
rolling hills of the Somme
To the genesis of the Western Front where
Belgium fell into the sea.
Here amongst the flooded dykes and
incomprehensible accents
He disappeared on patrol without a trace,
Vaporised by an obdurate shell.

'Regret to inform you...missing' said the telegram,
Words that through the pain and shock,
Hinted at hope – he could still be alive!
Clutching at straws – captured, memory loss,
She determined he would come home to her.
Consumed by this, even the later finality, 'presumed dead,'
Failed to dim this candle of hope –
Every knock at the door heralded his return
Every letter revived her dream.
Another war consumed her sons, one returned,
one dying at home,
But there was an almost satisfactory finality in this,
The presence of a grave left no room for hope.

The knocking at the door awoke the nurse,
she must have dozed
Sheepishly she approached the bed, but all was peaceful,
her face serene,
No longer did the knocking at the door matter,
It was over, her beloved was missing no longer

*Dedicated to the memory of Pte Frederick Henry Smith, 11th.
Border Regiment missing presumed dead 10.7.1917 and his
wife, Florence who until the end of her life believed he would
return.*

*N.B. 'The Pompadours' is the nickname of the Essex Regi-
ment from the colour of its facing when the regiment was
raised, which was puce, a colour named after the inventor of it
– the notorious Madame de Pompadour, mistress of Louis XV.*

The Letter

It had arrived some days ago, after the telegram
that shattered his world,
He saw it on the doormat, alerted by the rusty,
letter-box creaking.
Wanting to throw it away,
knowing it would only increase his heartbreak.
So studiously avoiding the hall,
he prayed it would disappear
Unsuccessfully pretending of its non-existence.
Until his sister called, tidied it up and put it on the table.
For hours he gazed at it,
the recent pain harshly re-awakened,
'We regret to inform you,'
five simple words that ended any happiness he ever had.
He was determined never to suffer it again –
It was six years since Arthur had gone with his blessing,
Only with the exhortation that he must write often,
To the land of opportunity, the land of hope.
Left in the house in which Arthur had been born and raised,
loved and treasured
Now a house without warmth or laughter.
Every week he wrote; unable to express his love,
or his emptiness,
Often gazing at the classroom photo, his only remembrance
of his son.
Arthur wrote little, he was disappointed, not surprised;
He had always avoided writing,
preferring to be active and adventurous..

He had to open the letter,
he knew he did and suddenly it was done.
Inside two letters, one in the educated hand of the Chaplain,
He barely noticed the words,
'Shot in the head.' 'He died instantly.' 'Felt no pain.'
The other in the hastily scribbled hand of Arthur,
dated June 6th
He opened with trembling hands and closely read the words,
Words with the shadow of doom upon them,
wiping a wayward tear,
Until it was finished and the words could hurt him no more.
Slipping from his hand it fell to the floor and
he repeated its final words,
'I shall always love you, Dad.'
As the waning fire spluttered one last time,
his head fell forward
On his chest, his body wracked by the tears withheld so long.

*Written on the occasion of my visit to the grave of Trooper
Arthur John HAILSTONE (641) 1st. Australian Light Horse,
Australian Imperial Forces, killed in action 7th. June 1915,
aged 22. and buried in Shrapnel Valley Cemetery.*

The Lie

"I lied to the vicar today," he blurted out suddenly.
She stopped eating, fork poised twixt plate and mouth.
It was so out of character, she could only gasp, "Why?"
Shocked at the enormity of the confession, she waited.
"I lied to him about my work on the memorial.
He asked me what was the most difficult part to carve
...and I lied.
It was easy to lie, I said the wreath of saffron crocuses,
But it was untrue."
She sat in silence, waiting, intrigued, but worried.
The wood on the fire crackled.
After what seemed an eternity, he slowly looked up,
"It was their names, Osborne and Archie," his voice broke,
"I finished them today and the emptiness of it hit me,
That's all that's left us, photos, memories and
Their names, just random letters carved in Portland stone."
She drew him to her and holding him close,
Together they wept silent tears.

The war memorial in Saffron Walden was built by the local firm of Whitehead and Day. Two of the late Mr. Osborne Whitehead's sons' names, Archibald and Osborne, are on it; Osborne was killed at Loos in 1915, Archibald three years later, in 1918 in Belgium. This poem is dedicated to all three of them.

The Live Bait Squadron

He dozed fitfully, middle-watch dragged;
The Hogue, old before her time, creaked,
An occasional snore escaped below;
The Broad Fourteens were still,
Nothing to report.
Ahead the Aboukir led the way,
Behind, last in the line of three, the Cressy.
He strained his eyes as dawn emerged,
Was Alexander looking at him
Or was he hammock bound?
Funny, he smiled, school friends
Same class at the Boys' British,
Then both in the 'Andrew,'
Since the outbreak, same squadron,
Same patrol, keeping the Hun away.

What were they – the Live Bait Squadron
'I bloody hope not', he thought,
But remembering the ancient Admiral's

Exhortation that submarines were 'playthings,'
His momentary doubt dissipated on a
Freshly awakened breeze.
His ruminations on coincidence and submarines
Were suddenly shattered by
A lone torpedo breaking Aboukir's back.
Glancing at his watch, 6.20 he noted
As the melee of launched life boats
Desperately sought souls to save,
But in twenty minutes she had gone.

Transfixed by the unfolding scene
It surprised him little
When two torpedoes hit amidships
Beneath his very feet.
Without panic he knew where to go
Alexander and the stationary Cressy
From whom lifeboats hunted
The human flotsam.
Clutching at the sanctuary of a lifebelt
He turned to see the Hogue
Disappear into the inky depths;
It was two hundred yards to safety
When horrified he saw the Cressy underway
At last aware of the lethal 'plaything.'

'Too late', he whispered to himself
As two torpedoes furrowed through the foam.
One missed; the other bludgeoned midships
On the starboard side
The old ship briefly retorted with her guns
But a third missile ruptured the engine-room
Scalding the slaving stokers.
He watched as lemming-like they jumped.
But as if in a dream he saw Alexander

On the foredeck, their eyes met,
He waved, as the Cressy rolled to starboard
And in fifteen minutes she, too was gone.
It was now 7.55.

Strangely content
Without insidious fear,
He felt the icy cold begin to overwhelm him,
The sea was unthreatening, placid
All was at peace, except
Occasional noises as the steam escaped;
A solitary plaintive cry of 'Mother,'
Then all was still... ..
He became aware of someone calling his name
Across the busy playground,
Turning he saw Alexander smiling,
Beckoning him to play
Waving back, happy not to be alone
He eagerly ran towards his friend;
As the immensity of the eternal ocean
Welcomed them into her bosom –
Friends in life, united in the fellowship of death.

In memory of Able-Seaman Errington Hounsome NORMAN (SS 2428) Royal Navy, H.M.S Hogue, drowned 22nd. September 1914, aged 27 and Leading-Seamen Alexander PERKIN (227224) Royal Navy, H.M.S Cressy, drowned 22nd. September 1915, aged 26, together in life and death.

The Loaded Dice

It snowed all night, desultory at first
Then enveloping everything –
The scars of battle, even death itself.
Later an incisive easterly wind persuaded the snow
Into a corner of the trench, cloyingly covering
The inherited French corpse, its horrors hidden.

Just before another deathly dawn,
A 'daily hate' peppered the trench
Killing three, wounding more.
It stopped, sated, as abruptly as it began
And lo the dormant snow had fled
Except in the poilu's sacred corner
Where head high it remained untouched,
An immaculate sanctuary.

Thus Fate chuckles as She throws her loaded dice.
An untouchable corner where raw elemental Death rules.

The Lost Sonata

She had been so beautiful, so ephemeral, her life full of music,
But a life alone and now she was gone, re-united
in celestial love.
At the bottom of a Venetian drawer they
found the faded score,
Written in the heat of battle so long ago,
performed, then forgotten.

From the hastily-dug Anzac trench
came the sound of humming,
Whistling, palpable above the cacophony
of the perpetual gunfire,
Even defying the constant droning of the bloated,
ever-present flies.
Nothing interrupted the music forming in his fertile mind.

He was oblivious to the trench,
the mayhem around him, everything
But the sequence of chords as they
came together on the page –
Not quite everything, the nascent
sonata shared the mental stage
With the recurring vision of his beautiful
Hungarian inspiration.

His concentration was finally broken
by a spasm of pain,
Legacy of Johnny Turk's shrapnel
which had creased his heel,

Painful enough, he had mused,
to thwart further Olympian ambition
As he thrust the finished score into his tunic pocket.

From the debacle of Gallipoli, recuperation
on leave in London
The first airing of the sonata, shared manifestation
of their love,
Until eschewing the opportunity of a 'cushy' staff post
He returned to the green rolling fields of death – the Somme.

November saw the winter closing in
with one last drive forward
A troublesome machine-gun post the target;
no shortage of volunteers.
He fell in no man's land a smile upon his face,
her image in his heart,
Music in his soul, his rendezvous with
death faced with equanimity.

Without him, nothing remained for her but performing, a life
Empty of everything but lonely memories and the music,
Played once at his requiem then
consigned to a seldom-opened drawer
The only tangible, but ever-present evidence, of their love.

He lies near where his love was snuffed out and
his music ceased forever,
Beneath a red sandstone monument,
midst the silent sepulchres of war.
His music, feared irretrievably lost in the
maelstrom of war, lives
Through the constancy of her love, conquering time and
death itself.

In Memory of Lieut-Commander Frederick Septimus 'Clegg,'
KELLY -Hood Battalion R.N. Div Royal Naval Volunteer
Reserve killed in action 13/11/1916,

D S C, Composer, Olympian, buried MARTINSART
BRITISH CEMETERY

And

JELLY D'ARANYI, Jelly Aranyi de Hunyadvár (Hungarian:
Hunyadvári Aranyi Jelly (30 May 1893 – 30 March 1966) –
Hungarian violinist.

The Lover Bullet

Unsteadily he clambered from the womb of the trench
Into the bright freedom of the field where the larks still sang
Suddenly it caressed him gently across the chest
And he fell back into the miasma of the enveloping mud.
The warmth of oozing sap cooled on his breast;
The darkness of the day suddenly pierced by
a keyhole of light
and there she was!

He held out his cold hand towards her remembered face
But as he grasped for her she faded slowly
Her eyes appealing, seducing him as so many times before
But then she was gone.

The insidious darkness slowly crept over all
And the clamour of battle held sway
As the orgasm of pain overwhelmed him
He clutched the release of death alone.

The Meakin Memorial

Midst the myriad meadows of mangelwurzels
Meakin of the Mortar Battery met his Maker
Mindful of the malevolent machine guns
He fell, and motionless
Merged into the malodorous mud.
His mortality remembered on the
Memorial to the Missing.
Marking the moment,
Making the memory remain,
His mourning sister made a monolithic memento.
Merciless time treated it malevolently
Until it needed moving to the margins.
Money would make this happen
But no merit in mediocrity, no momentary fame.
Only a mouldering enigmatic melancholy and
A manifest betrayal.

The Meakin Memorial is gradually falling to pieces in a field because it is too costly to move it and the WFA who should be trying to save it, are doing nothing, I think because there is little kudos in saving an old memorial unlike inaugurating a new one.

The Promised Land

The evening sun made the silver wings glow warmly
As they twisted, flipped and dived, the lifeline
of the fragile frame.
Homeward he was bound enraptured by the novelty,
The naïve pleasure of his first solo flight, he, child-like, played
Showing off to no appreciative audience but his own.
He had been to the stars and back, joyful and triumphant;
The boundless sky his playground, not to be shared.
Far better than the morass of trench life that he had forsaken,
Where the smell of death, of gas, of fear
haunted his very soul.
Inhabiting scars on the earth where the
sun never seemed to reach,
Pain, mutilation and death familiar acquaintances
Greeted every day round every muddy traverse.
But then they asked, to exchange the bowels of darkness
For the lightness of heaven, he hesitated not at all.
He knew insistent death would still seek him out
But to escape the confines of the earth... . .enough,
It seemed the answer, to live above the carnage,
to die in another dream.
Fear did not enter his cosmos, even though obliteration
Stalked them in training, he was a free spirit of the ether.
He turned into the sun as westwards was his base
Momentarily dazzled he shaded his eyes to dull the glare
But as he regained his sight a red
shadow passed across his view
A fusillade of angry bullets ripped into the flimsy frames,

That of the fragile aircraft, and his vulnerable body, too!
The pain induced a momentary spasm of crowded memories,'
But the darkness enveloped him and he saw a host of stars
As the plummeting coffin embraced the fields of Flanders
Exploding in a pyre-like ball of cleansing flame.

Inspired by the inscription on the grave of McCudden VC – 'Fly on dear boy from this dark world of strife, on to the promised land of eternal life.'

The Shard

It creased his brow with the permanence of death.
One of a searing blizzard of red-hot shards
That determinedly avoided his helmet
Slicing into him above the left eye
Stilling the throbbing fear of battle – forever.

Digging in the garden, the spade hit hard;
Not the usual flint offering,
But a simple slice of rusty metal.
He held it in his sweaty hand
Casually wondering at its provenance,
Never to know the unwilling target of
this now innocuous iron
Rested in the shaded village cemetery
Beneath the silent sentinel proclaiming.
'A British Soldier. Known unto God,'
- To God, and to this piece of commonplace inanimate metal!

The Veteran

Four a.m. the need to relieve an ancient bladder
He tottered in the inkyness towards the stairs
Unbalanced, he fell, the stairs rose up and all was black.
Dimly his view opened into the dug-out
The smell of ancient gas, his feet in fetid water.
Blood thumped in his head,
Shell on shell quivered and the earth moved.
Slowly he dragged his rag-doll body
Out of the trench slime
Out of the low-lying gas
Frantically drawing breath
Gulping at life, at light.
An oozing warmth – 'I've been hit',
Paralysed by fear.
Then a voice, encompassing arms around him
Picking up, gently admonishing,
'Come, Edwin, are you all right?
You must ring the bell, silly.'
The recurring nightmare fades
The safety of the bed beckons....
Till the curtains close again

The Weeds of Mourning

Nothing became her like the weeds of mourning;
Her angel-face mysterious behind the flimsy veil
The shapeless dress failing to disguise her perfect figure.
Men turned and stared, their first instinct, desire,
Then guilt and finally pity.

Women, jealous of her aura, turned away,
Muttering her grief was mere show, skin-deep
A device to snare another husband
As she had achieved before.

But what was she to do? Stop being pretty?
They did not know the rawness of the pain, her loss.
He had been her first, her only love
Sharing one night of joy before the cruel train
Took him away from her arms.

After the first letter, nothing except the emptiness
Shattered by the telegram, 'I regret to inform you....'
Valiantly, she carried on
Attempting to mask the depths of grief
Behind the uniform of widowhood.
Her life over.

But they were wrong!

'La Voix du Nord, Aout 1989 regrets to announce,' The death
of Mme P... aged 94, a widow whose husband disappeared on
the Aisne in Aout 1914....'

They Won't Tell!

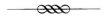

"….immediately, he felt no pain," the letter said.
It worked, an untruth kinder than the facts.
It was partly true, not a blatant lie,
The shell exploded and he was gone,
Vaporised, nothing left but a broken plate of false teeth.
He never wore them but carried them in his pocket.
A solitary man from the black streets of Burslem,
Unkempt, surly, a sorry soldier.
But no pain? Who knows.
He does, but will never tell, nor can his teeth!

Thiepval

Suddenly looking up from the small
world of his well-tilled garden,
The sound of contented bees busy in the lavender,
Where everything is defined by the perimeters of his plot,
He notices almost with shock, as if for the first time,
The great brick edifice astride the horizon.
Familiar as it is its presence looming there all his life
Yet today basking immoveable in the summer heat,
It seems immense, eternal, but ethereal
A gateway to a timeless world where the years mean nothing,
Where ageless faces stare out from family photos
Time locked cameos of another age.
Despite the haze the flags flow unfurled,
The pleasant breeze seeking them out
Fluttering proudly their shared hues of red, white and blue.
The field between his horticultural cosmos and the monument
Bears the hidden footprints of those who fell,
Gentle, green gratifying the stolid cattle grazing,
Can they see the ghostly lines of stoical khaki

Steadily advancing to where the chateau once stood?
Now the flags wave proudly
Above the litany of simple names of those who fell,
Immortalised in inscribed stone
Evidence of their sacrifice in those long ago killing fields.
Tomorrow when he wakes it will still be there
When he has gone, the garden neglected, a wilderness,
It will remain, redbrick and resolute,
redolent of Remembrance – THIEPVAL

Truffles

At home it would soon be time for the truffles,
Giacomo, day-dreamed,
waiting in the shallow trench
Under a relentless summer sun.
The heat was not a trial for him,
Born under the tower of Frederick
On one of the three small hills of San Miniato.
Ah, but the truffles, another thing, how he loved them;
But for the Ragazzi del '99, he would be safe at home,
Anticipating his marriage to the dark-eyed Francesca,
The envy of all his friends, a real beauty,
Whose father was the finest truffle hunter
In the Arno valley.
But now, the future was unknown;
Italy was on her knees;
The losses had to be replenished,
and he was eighteen,
Conscripted and known as the
'Boys of 99', hastily trained

He went to the Piave front singing,
eager to prove his patriotism
Even forgetful of the truffles –for a moment.
Now waiting, unafraid, he mused on the irony –
San Miniato, in deepest Toscana,
with its strange sobriquet
An unpatriotic 'Al Tedesco,' 'To the German,'
As the smell of the truffles
Embraced his memory again.

Tuscan Twilight

As he dozed on the verandah in the big chair he so loved,
The sun's fire had faded and
a gentle breeze caressed the greenery,
His arthritis was never easy now,
and he blamed it on that stinking country,
Scene of his first campaign with the legion, so long ago.
The fierce heat of a Tuscan summer was coming to an end;
His cool old house, bought with his praemic
as a retiring legionnaire,
A haven amidst the vineyards,
where he would live out his days –
After forty years' service, man and boy,
in Gaul, Jerusalem and Britain.
Oh, cursed Britain, where the natives aped the beasts,
painted their bodies;
More chance of educating the animals of
their impenetrable forests!
How he had hated the never-ending rain;
the sky like sullen death,

Where the sun became a distant memory, where savages
stalked the shadows.

At the age of sixteen he had left his Tuscan heartland,
shaped by its benevolent sun;
Tearful farewells to his distraught mother,
father grim-faced, but proud,
Proud his only son had chosen the way of the
legion as he and his father before.
When after all those years he returned, affluent, a little fatter,
With memories to share with those
who would listen, his parents were dead;
The farm under the cypresses a ruin, no-one to listen, all had
gone, or had forgotten him.

Many a day on that far-flung wall
as the drizzle soaked him to the skin,
The mist inexorably rolling in from that blasted land,
He was tempted to dream of home,
but vigilance here was a deathly business,
The fearsome Pict had no scruples, just kill and maim,
Usually the removal of testicles, before the roughly slit throat!
Suddenly with a start he saw Tiberius' smiling
face in his mind's eye;
The first time in years that he had thought of him,
remembering with a shiver
How they found his shattered body, blood-soaked throat,
and beneath his tunic... . .
How he hated those beasts whom humanity had passed by.

Teutoburg Forest was where he came of age,
in the primeval forests of death,
Where the cruel Gaul was a fearsome, ferocious foe –
But he had survived, earned promotion, posted to the
Empire's corners,

Until his time was up when a farm in Britain
was offered for his dotage;
A farm amidst the heathen wilderness
where the rain never ceased.
But it could not be so, the Tuscan sun was
branded into his very soul.
So he returned, his only baggage his memories and the dark-
skinned slave girl,
Booty from Nubia, whom one day he found he loved.
Returned to the vines, the cypresses, the sun.
And he was content, apart from that damned British arthritis!

He dozed on the verandah in the big chair he so loved,
The sun had gone behind the hill now, the breeze had stilled;
The soft golden light suffused the scene foretelling another
scorching day –
Another day when memories would hold sway.

Via Dolorosa

The march of time means nothing to the dead.
The perpetual pilgrims on the sacred way of remembrance
Are unchanging in their purpose
But ever different in their means.
The Via Dolorosa to Flanders' shrines
Echoes down the well-trodden years
From those familiar with the empty chair at home
To the quest for a stone-carved name
Written in faded pencil upon the sepia snap.

Away from these public cathedrals
From secluded Authuille to lonely Zouave Valley
The heart-rending confessional is recited
Of love, of honour, of respect
To those who chose the sacred way of duty
And died upon the Calvary of war
For us.

Voie Sacree

Startled he awoke as the laden lorry lurched
into another mud-filled hole,
Simultaneously a rogue shell burst on the
lumbering lorry ahead;
The air was rent with screams of men and beast,
The windscreen mud-spattered, now crimson with gore.
Within minutes the ruptured vehicle was pushed aside;
The ghastly wounded hurried away;
the dead left to await retrieval;
The shattered horses roughly tipped into adjacent craters
To fester and bloat until the quick-lime was spread.

It mattered little as long as most of
this perpetual transport
Delivered its sacred cargo- supplies
and men to the end of the line;
Cannon-fodder to fuel the sacrifice in the hell called Verdun.
'Ils ne passeront pas,' even, it seemed,
till every last man in France must die.

Every day in the early Spring two thousand
lorries plodded each way
An interminable immortal lifeline.
Carrying an army of men to the sacrificial fields;
Whilst another phantom army stood by to
ensure the sacred road open.

Gerard's musings were interrupted as
the truck lurched into life
Continuing the inexorable journey to disgorge
more fuel for the battle.
Only three short hours till the fun began,
why worry you'll die anyway!
Here, selfishly, he felt safe, piniored
between the fat baker, Pascal from Paris,
And the stolid frame of the Norman farmer, Guillaume.
Protection from all but a lucky direct hit.
He reprimanded himself for such un-comradely thoughts,
But war had taught him one thing if nothing else –
take care of number one.
He dozed fitfully, the steady rain dripping off his helmet,
Down his neck, sending a shiver, not of fear, but of cold,
through him.
A hint of a grim-smile creased his lips,
Only another ten kilometres of fear to arrive in Hell,
Only another hour to go, of this, and probably life itself.

The Village Wedding

The parish church slumbers in the early sunshine.
The day yet to rouse itself from summer lethargy,
The bright blooms turn their heads to greet the sun's warmth.
Unchanged and unchanging the dawn chorus, eager, bracing,
Ecstatically greets the advent of another day.
From Saxon times through wars, peace, want and abundance
The ancient pile had witnessed all, a silent spectator,
A haven and the bedrock of the villagers' lives.

Today another scene from the folio of life –
A joining of two kindred spirits in love and happiness.
The old edifice stretched, creaked and yawned
Happy that one of its children, after many a journey
Has returned to her rural roots with someone eager
To share this bucolic paradise.

The day grows warmer; the sounds of expectant merriment
Float on the soft breeze from the ancient hostelry
Across the Pelham road to the slowly filling church.

The revellers, dressed in summer finery
Enter the cool, sacred nave, calmed by the gentle music;
Laughter settles and anticipation quickens the pulse.

Nearby a cottage door opens and pretty as a
sunbeam the bride appears
Arm in arm with her Punch-proud father,
Greeted with delight as they stroll the short walk whilst
Inside the hushed church the happy groom
calmly looks around
As whispered information announces the arrival of the bride.

Entering by the south, sun-filled door, the organ promulgates;
The congregation rise as one, craning over their shoulders;
The old church radiates harmony and their journey together
through Life, nurtured on love and friendship, begins
Bathed in the sunshine of hope and the
steadfast strength of love –
Kate and Ben.

Lightning Source UK Ltd.
Milton Keynes UK
UKOW04n1435010515

250751UK00001B/3/P